New Life SERIES

From Guest to Disciple

Joel D. Heck

CPH.
Concordia Publishing House

Edited by Thomas J. Doyle

Copyright © 2001 Concordia Publishing House
3558 S. Jefferson Avenue, St. Louis, MO 63118-3968

This publication is available in braille and in large print for the visually impaired. Write to the Library for the Blind, 1333 S. Kirkwood Rd., St. Louis, MO 63122-7295; or call 1-800-433-3954.

1　2　3　4　5　6　7　8　9　10　　　　　10　09　08　07　06　05　04　03　02　01

Contents

This book is dedicated
to the hospitable pastor
and people of Immanuel
Lutheran Church, Winnipeg,
Manitoba, whose 1996
Conference on Evangelism served
as the catalyst for this book,
and to Joseph Aldrich, whose
provocative statements in his
book _Lifestyle Evangelism_
provided the initial idea.

I would also like to acknowledge
the many insightful suggestions
from two very fine readers,
Erwin J. Kolb and Dan
Paavola. Their comments have
enriched the book and made it
more consistent, readable, and
enjoyable.

Session 1 Love Them Until They Ask You Why

*W*hen there is room in the heart there is room in the *house*. Danish Proverb

This book intends to bring evangelism within the reach of every concerned Christian. Most people will think that impossible, but with God nothing is impossible (Mark 10:27). In fact, the major problem with many approaches to evangelism is that they are beyond the reach of most Christians. Friendship approaches to evangelism, sometimes called lifestyle evangelism or relational evangelism, have brought the evangelistic task closer to the typical Christian, but a gap remains.

The very word *evangelism* frightens many Christians, and the thought of actually talking to someone about the Christian faith does likewise. But if it were possible to bring evangelism within the reach of every concerned Christian, wouldn't many Christians be relieved? Wouldn't many Christians take a look? Wouldn't many Christians actually consider, seriously, the possibility of reaching out to those outside the Christian faith? Wouldn't many Christians even invite non-Christians into their homes, get acquainted with them, meet their needs, and build a friendship? And might some of those Christians, who have never considered talking about their faith, actually talk about their faith as a result? I believe so. The following paragraphs will provide a glimpse into the way in which that can occur.

Joseph Aldrich, author, conference speaker, and president of Multnomah School of the Bible in Portland, Oregon, tells this story:

> I recently met a fascinating, radiant Christian from India. His ministry to international students is leading scores of Hindus and Moslems to Christ. What accounts for his effectiveness in reaching members of these radically different cultural and religious traditions?
>
> Each Sunday, he told me, he and his wife host somewhere between thirty and fifty students for dinner. That's a key part of his strategy. Food and camaraderie break down barriers. There's

7

something about eating a meal with someone that accelerates friendship.

"So you talk about Christ at these meals?" I asked.

"No," he said. "It is impossible to talk openly of Jesus Christ."

" So how," I asked him, "are you able to see so many find Christ?"

"I love them," he replied, "until they ask me why." ...

"Through loving them," he continued, "they meet Jesus Christ, even though they don't know whom they've met. Once they've sensed the reality of his love through me, they're open to discuss the reason for the love and acceptance they've experienced."

Excerpted from the book *Gentle Persuasion: Creative Ways to Introduce Your Friends to Christ* by Joseph Aldrich (Portland: Multnomah Press, 1988), 8.

"I love them until they ask me why." What a great motto for the Christian witness! What a great title for a book on evangelism, or at least a session! The purpose of this book is to encourage you to love them until they ask you why by practicing hospitality. You need not do it in the way that Indian Christian did. You need not do it with international students or with Hindus and Muslims. But find your own unique way to love them until they ask you why. We'll talk about how to do that later, but the gathering of people around the dinner table in the above story gives us a glimpse at one of the many possible methods and, indeed, one of the most effective methods.

But think about this concept for a moment. Love them until they ask you why. That's exactly what God did for us. He loved us so much that He gave His Son to die for us. "But God demonstrates His own love for us in this: While we were still sinners, Christ died for us" (Romans 5:8). In our clear moments, we sometimes ask Him why. The only answer we hear, when we listen carefully in the reading of His Word, is His love for us, His grace to us, His undeserved kindness in Christ Jesus. He loves us, and sometimes we ask, "Why do You love me so much, Lord?" Knowing ourselves as well as we do, we know our sin, our shortcomings, and our failures. We wonder how anyone could love us. But God does, always, and He loves all people, including those who are not yet a part of His flock (John 10:16). He would use us by His grace and according to His sovereign will to reach them.

This book is about loving the people around us. Some would

classify this book, correctly, as a book on friendship evangelism. Friendship evangelism has to do with sharing one's faith in Jesus Christ within the context of a growing relationship rather than in the form of a proclamation from the pulpit, an evangelism visit, a crusade, or another approach to outreach. Friendship evangelism is generally not confrontational. Friendship evangelism, of course, involves two elements—talking about Jesus Christ (evangelism) and a growing relationship with another person (friendship). While many other books deal with the former and a number touch on the latter, few books I have encountered even approach the topic of helping people to think through how to develop that relationship by means of hospitality. That is the purpose of this book—to demonstrate the value of hospitality for outreach.

This book will not traverse the same ground covered in other books on friendship evangelism. You may already know about Win Arn's insight in his book *The Master's Plan for Making Disciples* (Church Growth Press) on the importance of friendship for new Christians—he emphasizes that a new Christian should have at least six friends in the church. You may have read the books of Joseph Aldrich or Rebecca Pippert. You may even be familiar with the comment of Elmer Towns, "Relationships are the glue that make people stick to the church."[1] This book will move from those insights to chart new territory.

In session 2, you will read about the key New Testament passages that speak of the importance of hospitality, but you will also learn about the extensive practice of hospitality in both the Old and New Testaments. In session 3, you will especially discover how important hospitality was for the ministry of Jesus. Session 4 will discuss whether or not hospitality is a spiritual gift, and the final two sessions will get very practical. Session 5 will suggest that Christians can practice hospitality on three levels—the personal level (the most obvious level), the congregational level (churches can be hospitable), and the community level (especially having to do with meeting needs in the community). Session 6 will show you what the practice of hospitality looks like in several different congregations and what it could perhaps look like in your congregation.

One of the benefits of a friendship evangelism approach is that people who become Christians through such an approach are more likely to stay in the church. In other words, new Christians are more

9

effectively assimilated when relationships are built with these people prior to their coming to faith and uniting with a church.

The original impetus for this book is Joseph Aldrich, not just because of his story about the Indian Christian. Many years ago, while teaching an introductory course on evangelism, I read these words in Aldrich's book *Lifestyle Evangelism* about the keys to sharing the Christian faith within one's lifestyle: "A fourth key," he wrote, "is *to invite them to your home.* Your goal is to advance your backyard-fence relationship toward a more significant friendship. Meals are a great way to do it."[2] What an intriguing concept, I thought. And that was my springboard, one that took me a long time to decide to jump on and spring from. The people and pastor of Immanuel Lutheran Church, Winnipeg, Manitoba, motivated me to jump, but more about them later.

Ted Engstrom gives us an example of his own exercise of the gift of hospitality. In his book *The Fine Art of Friendship,* he tells the story of Khang Lee. Khang Lee and his wife, Thu, were Buddhists who became acquainted with Engstrom during the 1960s in South Vietnam as a result of Engstrom's work with World Vision. The Lees helped World Vision do its work as effectively as possible, and they often had Engstrom into their home.

When it became clear that South Vietnam would not win the Vietnam War, Khang and his wife made a plan for their evacuation. If they became separated during evacuation and they both lived, they would try to contact Ted Engstrom in the United States. Eventually they were reunited in the States with Engstrom's help. World Vision sponsored them and helped them adjust to life in a new country.

Then one day, after some time in his new country, Khang Lee said, "Mr. Ted, I want to become a Christian. But I don't want to do it because you helped me. I will do it because I want Jesus to be in my life."

The Engstroms and the Lees got acquainted in Khang Lee's home, and they became further acquainted after the war in Ted and Dorothy Engstrom's home. Clearly hospitality was not a one-way street; the Engstroms were both the recipients of hospitality and the givers of hospitality. While much happened in the process—needs were met, cooperation in the work of World Vision occurred, the faith was shared—the setting for much of this was the home. Engstrom comments:

Khang and I started out with seemingly nothing in common. He was a Vietnamese officer; I was with World Vision. He was Buddhist, and I was Christian. Our homes were thousands of miles apart. We spoke different languages, ate different foods, and espoused different world views. Nevertheless our mutual respect and willingness to accept each other as equals made all the difference. It provided the framework for us to become friends.

Excerpted from *The Fine Art of Friendship: Building and Maintaining Quality Relationships* by Theodore Wilhelm Engstrom with Robert C. Larson (Nashville: Thomas Nelson, 1985), 81–83.

In short, he loved Khang Lee until Khang asked him why.

We who believe that Jesus died for us have the privilege of demonstrating that in our lives, of becoming "the aroma of Christ among those who are being saved" (2 Corinthians 2:15).

Joseph Aldrich says, "Christians are to be good news before they share the good news."[3] Dick Innes says, "We need therefore to *be* God's person before we *do* God's work, and thereby establish our credibility to verify our message."[4] The practice of hospitality enables us, to be good news, to be God's person, and to establish our credibility and thereby verify our message. Throughout the rest of this book, you will learn about the biblical foundation for hospitality and the many practical ways in which you can practice hospitality toward the non-Christians whom God brings within your circle of acquaintance. One of those ways is to invite them into your home, like the Indian Christian does, but many other possibilities exist.

Discussion

1. "But God demonstrates His own love for us in this: While we were still sinners, Christ died for us" (Romans 5:8). Think about that passage. What does it say? What does it mean? What does it mean to you?

2. The primary New Testament word for hospitality, *philoxenia,* occurs twice in the New Testament (Romans 12:13 and Hebrews 13:2). The related adjective *philoxenos,* "hospitable, given to hospitality," occurs three times in the New Testament (1 Timothy 3:2, Titus 1:8, 1 Peter 4:9). Look up each passage and record your insights.
Romans 12:13

   1 Timothy 3:2

   Titus 1:8

   Hebrews 13:2

   1 Peter 4:9

3. The primary word for *hospitality* in the New Testament is actually made up of a verb meaning "to love" and the word for stranger. Relate that etymology to the following Bible passage: "We love because He first loved us" (1 John 4:19). What is our motivation?

4. Read the following hymn stanzas. Where does God choose to take up residence? What does this say about God? What does this say about the hymn writers?

"O Little Town of Bethlehem," *LW* 59, stanza 3:

How silently, how silently The wondrous gift is giv'n!
So God imparts To human hearts The blessings of His heav'n.
No ear may hear His coming; But in this world of sin,
Where meek souls will Receive Him,
still The dear Christ enters in.

"Lift Up Your Heads," *LW* 23, stanza 3:

O happy town, O blessed land
That keeps our gracious King's command,
And blest the heart when He comes in His holy
reign there to begin.
His entrance is the dawn of bliss;
He fills our lives and makes them His.
Our highest praise we bring, God, Comforter and King.

"From Heaven Above to Earth I Come," *LW* 38, stanza 5:

O dearest Jesus, holy child,
Prepare a bed, soft, undefiled,
A holy shrine, within my heart,
That you and I need never part.

What is the significance of the fact that these hymns belong to the Advent or Christmas season?

5. Read Luke 14:12–14. What does this section of Scripture suggest about the ministry of Jesus? How did Jesus model the teaching he offered in these verses? Are the poor, the crippled, and so on exclusively those who are literally poor, or might there be some other meaning?

Endnotes

1. Larry Gilbert, "Small Group Evangelism: Using AMEs and RSAs to Reach People for Christ," *Church Growth Institute Newsletter* 1, no. 12, p. 8.

2. Joseph Aldrich, *Lifestyle Evangelism: Learning to Open Your Life to Those Around You* (Sisters, Oreg.: Questar Publishers), 179.

3. Aldrich, *Lifestyle Evangelism,* 19.

4. Dick Innes, "Witnessing: A Way of Life or a Way with Words?" *Christianity Today* 28 (May 18, 1984): 45.

Session 2 Hospitality Begins with Love

*H*ospitality is one form of worship. *Jewish Proverb*

Hospitality: Love for the Stranger

So what does the Bible, especially the New Testament, say about hospitality? Five key passages in the New Testament contain some form of the primary word for hospitality, and to those passages we will turn shortly. First, we look at a brief listing of the passages.

The New Testament word for hospitality, *philoxenia,* occurs twice in the New Testament (Romans 12:13 and Hebrews 13:2). The related adjective *philoxenos,* "hospitable, given to hospitality," occurs three times in the New Testament (1 Timothy 3:2; Titus 1:8; 1 Peter 4:9). We will come back to these five passages later.

The primary word for *hospitality* in the New Testament is actually made up of a verb meaning "to love," *phileo,* and the word for stranger, *xenos* (*philoxenia* when combined, "love for the stranger"). Consequently, both the word *hospitality* and the concept of hospitality begin with love! God invites us to love those strangers until they ask us why. Those who love strangers are those who show hospitality in one sense or another. Those who love strangers enough to want them to become a part of the kingdom of God can show hospitality and share their faith within the exercise of that hospitality.

That shouldn't surprise us. Everything that a Christian is and does begins with love. God created us because He loves us. When we fell away in sin, He sent us a Savior because He loves us. When we trust in His gracious forgiveness, God in His great love has brought us there. When we respond to this love, we follow His example and are motivated by the love God showed when Jesus died on the cross for the sins of the world. "We love because He first loved us" (1 John 4:19). When we live our lives conscious of God's grace, "Love does no harm to its neighbor. Therefore love is

15

the fulfillment of the law" (Romans 13:10). If all of that is true, and it is, then the practice of hospitality, when properly motivated, flows from the love of God. Hospitality begins with love.

But when we talk about the love of God for us, our love for God, and our love for one another, we are talking about several types of love. The Greek word *phileo* is just one of those types of love, related, of course, to the others. Therefore, before we look closely at the five passages, let's take a quick look at one of the books that C. S. Lewis penned. He wrote a book called *The Four Loves*. In that book he discussed four Greek words for love, and his discussion clarifies for us the difference between the various loves. It would be a mistake for us to assume that early Christians had just one word for love, the same word that is used of marital love, of God's love for us, and of our love for our fellow human beings.

According to Lewis, *storge* (the English word *affection* is a close synonym) is the first one, the "humblest and most widely diffused of loves, the love in which our experience seems to differ least from that of the animals."[1] *Philia* (the noun form here for consistency in this paragraph, meaning "friendship") is the second, a love that we can manage to live without, a love that is least likely to be jealous. *Eros* (romantic love) is the third with its focus on love between the sexes, especially in marriage. *Agape* (charity) is the fourth, an unselfish kindness toward others. *Agape* and the related verb *agapao* are used 269 times in the New Testament. *Agapao* is the verb used in John 3:16: "For God so *loved* the world …" If one thinks of a pyramid, *storge* is at the bottom, *philia* the next rung up, *eros* the third level, and *agape* the top level, each of them rising to a higher expression of love.

The first three are natural loves, human loves, and the fourth is divine love. The first three must be transformed by divine love, or they become corrupted. Hence, we see the importance of our hospitality being motivated and informed by God's love for us in Christ. But we also see that hospitality, a combination of the words *phileo,* "to love," and *xenos,* "stranger," fits into the friendship category. Hospitality is not to be confused with any of the other three. Hospitality does not, first and foremost, involve affection or marital love or divine love. Hospitality can become the vehicle for the expression of affection and for the communication of divine love, but hospitality, *friendship* with the stranger, must be informed by the love of God in Christ at the cross in order to have value for outreach. In other words, God must shape us so that we may work the work of God through our hospitality and our witness. God is the host; we are His guests. He is the initiator; we are the respondents.

According to the *Theological Dictionary of the New Testament* (9:115), the "most likely basic sense" of *phileo,* "to love," is the idea of "proper to," or "belonging to."[2] This means that someone who loves another in the sense of friendship is one who relates well to that person, that is, is "proper to" that person. The word *phileo* in its original sense, then, means "to regard and treat somebody as one of one's own people" (*Theological Dictionary of the New Testament* 9:115). Another way of saying this is in the form of the Golden Rule: "So in everything, do to others what you would have them do to you, for this sums up the Law and the Prophets" (Matthew 7:12).

The word *phileo* applies to the love of parents for children, spouses for one another, masters for servants, and people for their nation or city. The word is especially used for the love of friends for one another. The *Theological Dictionary of the New Testament* (9:116) tells us that *phileo* can mean "to help," "to care for," "to treat as a guest," "to entertain." This word for love means "to do what is proper to" the object of our love, "what is natural for him" (*Theological Dictionary of the New Testament* 9:117).

There is also a very large number of words in the New Testament compounded from the Greek *phil-*. The verb *phileo* and compounds occur twenty-five times in the New Testament. The verb is not always neatly distinguished from *agapao,* the word for divine love, which suggests the proximity of friendship to divine love.

This word for love, *phileo,* is so prominent in the New Testament that six New Testament names carry the word *love, phil-,* within them: Philemon (Philemon 1), Philetus (2 Timothy 2:17), Philip (Mark 3:18), Philologus (Romans 16:15), Philippi (Acts 16:12), and Philadelphia (Revelation 1:11, 3:7).

According to the *Theological Dictionary of the New Testament* (9:147), a *philos* (another noun derived from the verb "to love") is a "friend." When combined with the ideas for hospitality, *phileo* means "to entertain." Ancient authors wrote a great deal on friendship. Real friendship is possible only with a few. The true ideal is the pair of friends. The supreme duty of a friend is to sacrifice oneself for the friend, even to the point of death. Jesus said, "Greater love has no one than this, that he lay down his life for his friends" (John 15:13). The philosopher Aristotle (384–322 B.C.) said in his

Ethica Nichomachea (9.8), "To a noble man there applies the true saying that he does all things for the sake of his friends … and, if need be, he gives his life for them." The Epicurean Philonides (second century B.C.) said in his *Vitus Philonidis* (22), "For the one he loved most among those close to him or friends he was ready to offer his neck." Socrates (ca. 470–399 B.C.) is reported to have told others to follow the example of Apollo, who allegedly chased a man out of the temple who did not come to the aid of his friend when in mortal danger (Epictetus, *Enchiridion,* 32.3). To approach this kind of love in the exercise of hospitality is to live outside oneself, to love another.

This is precisely where the failure to practice hospitality will show up—in the lack of love for those in need, in a love that is primarily self-serving rather than serving. The high value we place on individual choice, individual happiness, and the other manifestations of individualism in America today works against us. Concern for those in need and for those outside the Christian faith are a part of every Christian's thinking by the power of the Holy Spirit, and thinking outside ourselves is a part of the Spirit's work in us. Only when sin has its way with us is it otherwise.

The English Word *Hospitality*

We have looked at the Greek behind the word *hospitality.* Now let's look at the English word *hospitality* and its related words. The English word is defined by *Webster's Third New International Dictionary* as "the cordial and generous reception and entertainment of guests or strangers socially or commercially." A second meaning is "ready receptivity especially to new ideas and interests." As some dictionaries will show, the following words are all etymologically related: *host, hospice, hospital, hospitality, hospitable, hostel,* and *hotel.* They all come from a word that means "one who provides lodging or entertainment for a guest or visitor."

Five Key Passages

The most important New Testament passages are the five that contain the adjective *philoxenos,* "hospitable," or the noun *philoxenia,* "hospitality." We must mine these passages in order to understand the concept of hospitality. Three of them are from the pen of

Paul, who must have been very dependent upon the hospitality of others. One of them is from Peter, and one from the writer to the Hebrews.

1. "Share with God's people who are in need. Practice *hospitality"* (Romans 12:13).
2. "Now the overseer must be above reproach, the husband of but one wife, temperate, self-controlled, respectable, *hospitable,* able to teach" (1 Timothy 3:2).
3. "Rather he [an overseer] must be *hospitable,* one who loves what is good, who is self-controlled, upright, holy and disciplined" (Titus 1:8).
4. "Do not forget *to entertain strangers,* for by so doing some people have entertained angels without knowing it" (Hebrews 13:2).
5. "*Offer hospitality* to one another without grumbling" (1 Peter 4:9).

Romans 12:13

Share with God's people who are in need. Practice hospitality.
Romans 12:13

In this verse a natural pair of ideas focus inwardly: fellowship and hospitality. The word translated "share" is related to the word *fellowship.* Fellowship has to do with contributing to the needs of the saints; it addresses the conduct of Christian people, and only Christian people, when they come together. It flows out of the relationship of believers to one another within the body of Christ. Fellowship has to do with the mutual gathering of people, none of whom is the host, none of whom is spiritually lost.

Hospitality, on the other hand, has to do with the gathering of people when one person or group is the host and the other is the guest. In the case of biblical fellowship, all of the participants are believers. In the case of hospitality, all may be believers or some may be believers and others not. The host might be the believers and the guests non-Christians, or the host might be non-Christian and the guests Christian. When we are the hosts, we need to treat others as guests, whether they are believers or not. Non-Christians, even if they despise us or ridicule us, need to be treated as guests. Perhaps this is why Solomon writes, "If your enemy is hungry, give him food to eat; if he is thirsty, give him water to drink. In doing

19

this, you will heap burning coals on his head, and the LORD will reward you" (Proverbs 25:21–22). True Christian hospitality toward the non-Christian may break through that rough exterior and reach the heart.

The reason why fellowship and hospitality form a natural pair is that hospitality is an aspect of fellowship, growing out of the general, biblical concept of fellowship. Part of fellowship is hospitality. In other words, hospitality is an expression of the larger concept of fellowship. Both have to do with the gathering of people. Both, therefore, have a social dimension. Both seek to enrich the people gathered. But in the practice of hospitality the church cannot reach out in the practice of fellowship. Therefore, *fellowship evangelism* is an oxymoron.[3] However, if I could paraphrase Paul, I would say, "The important thing is that in every way, whether with appropriate terminology or inappropriate, Christ is preached. And because of this I rejoice" (see Philippians 1:18). Since Paul says "in every way," I have no real quarrel with the phrase *fellowship evangelism.*

According to this verse and the entire Scripture, hospitality is one of the most important Christian duties.

> The Christians looked upon themselves as a body of men scattered throughout the world, living as aliens amongst strange people, and therefore bound together as the members of a body, as the brethren of one family. The practical realization of this idea would demand that whenever a Christian went from one place to another he should find a home among the Christians in each town he visited.[4]

Sometimes, hospitality was urgently necessary because persecution forced these early Christians to migrate. Though the world was inhospitable, believers must not be. Martin Franzmann writes, "'Hospitality' would be a special form of this active, sympathetic helpfulness, for hospitality is thought of here not as a general social graciousness but as a form of aid to be supplied to travelers, especially to exiled or persecuted fellow Christians."[5]

To "practice hospitality" means here "to follow after or pursue hospitality." It implies that we are to actively pursue hospitality and not just bestow it when circumstances make it unavoidable. The English word *practice* in this context translates a New Testament word that means to pursue. Therefore, pursue hospitality, not as one window-shops, but as one hunts an animal. Love the stranger, therefore, not haphazardly or when convenient, but at every opportunity, even if the stranger is in a bad mood. It is not optional, but an integral part of the Christian lifestyle. R. C. H. Lenski in his interpretation of Paul's epistle to the Romans writes that "a whole chapter would be needed to set forth this 'hospitality' ... as it was practiced in the early church... . It was the regular thing in the case of Christians."[6] Jesus emphasizes this idea in another way when he tells us, "Love your enemies" (Matthew 5:44), and go the extra mile for people other than your friends (Matthew 5:38–42).

Notice that Romans 12:13 appears within the same chapter as one of the recognized lists of spiritual gifts (Romans 12:4–8). Later we will discuss whether or not hospitality is a spiritual gift. At this point, we suggest that its proximity to spiritual gifts at least argues for its importance and usefulness. Actually, more important is the appearance of Romans 12:13 shortly after the command to love (12:9). As was pointed out earlier, hospitality literally means "love for the stranger." Hospitality is one way to express that love.

As to the outreach dimension of Romans 12:13, most commentators see no concern for the non-Christian in the verse. The verse focuses God's people. Verse 10 of the same chapter uses the phrase "one another," which usually refers to believers. However, the word *hospitality* literally translates as "love for the *stranger.*" There is no necessary reason for us to limit the concept of the stranger to the non-Christian stranger. To say that a verse focuses on the believer is one thing, but to say that this focus excludes the outsider is to say more than the text says. The Greek word for *hospitality* is not that precise. Though this verse in Romans 12 seems to be inwardly directed, certainly the entire New Testament is much concerned about the person outside the family of faith. Indeed, our understanding of hospitality above suggests that the host may be host to both believer and unbeliever. As Paul reminds us elsewhere, "Therefore, as we have opportunity, let us do good to all people, especially to those who belong to the family of believers" (Galatians 6:10), but not exclusively to those who belong to the family of believers.

1 Timothy 3:2

Now the overseer must be above reproach, the husband of but one wife, temperate, self-controlled, respectable, hospitable, able to teach. 1 Timothy 3:2

21

Years ago, my wife's pastor wrote to her entire high school graduating class, congratulating them on the completion of that step in their education. Their church had two events planned in their honor. The first was recognition of the class in a Sunday worship service, and the second was an evening in the home of the pastor. She remembers that pastor as the most effective pastor of her early years, and the hospitality that he and his wife demonstrated was undoubtedly a part of that effectiveness. He must have read 1 Timothy 3:2.

This passage is part of a list of qualifications for pastors, so, once again, the focus is primarily on the believer. The "overseer" is one who administers the work of others, while working himself. Lea and Griffin echo the thoughts of the commentators cited above:

> In relation to other believers Christians needed to be "hospitable." Traveling Christian groups (3 John 5–8) would be dependent upon the kindness of local Christians as they passed through communities while spreading the Gospel. The task of caring for Christians and other "strangers" was highly respected in both Christian and Greek culture (Rom[ans] 12:13; 1 Tim[othy] 5:10; 1 Pet[er] 4:9).[7]

This was a day when social welfare was virtually nonexistent, when widows and orphans were dependent on their relatives, persecutions were fierce, poverty and hunger were in evidence, and lodging with unbelievers less than desirable. Lenski in his commentary underscores the basic idea: "It does not mean to entertain and to feast friends or even the poor but to take in Christian strangers or acquaintances when these are traveling, or when they are fleeing from persecutions and often are without means of any kind."[8]

Donald Wayne Riddle writes about Papias, possible disciple of the apostle John and the bishop of Hierapolis in the second century A.D., who obeyed this injunction of Paul and in the practice of hospitality inquired about the disciples and others who had been with Jesus so that he might learn more about them.[9]

Lenski's comment does not mean that there is no outreach dimension intended in this verse, either by the specific concern for being hospitable or in the general qualifications of pastors. What pastor could claim to be faithful to the message of the Gospel if he was not concerned about sharing that message with the unbeliever?

In fact, in 1 Timothy 3:7, Paul writes that the overseer must have a good reputation with outsiders, so the non-Christian is in view here, though not prominent.

Joseph Aldrich writes about the leaders who reach out and share their faith, "Finally, our model leader is to be hospitable, a 'lover of strangers' (1 Tim[othy] 3:2; Titus 1:8). We should remember to extend hospitality to strangers (Heb[rews] 13:2) and to invite guests home for dinner (Rom[ans] 12:13). The leader's home circle is to be an open circle."[10]

Titus 1:8

> **Rather he must be hospitable, one who loves what is good, who is self-controlled, upright, holy and disciplined. Titus 1:8**

Like the previous passage, this occurrence of the word *hospitable* is also found in one of the lists of qualifications for pastors. Lea and Griffin write in their commentary on 1 and 2 Timothy and Titus that the overseer must be hospitable, "devoted to the welfare of others," someone who would "entertain Christian *or non-Christian visitors* on behalf of the church."[11] They also write that hospitality "was a thoroughgoing expectation of all Christians in the early church."[12] Here, especially, a leader is encouraged to be ready to befriend and to lodge destitute, traveling, or persecuted believers. Again, one should gladly open house and home to traveling or persecuted Christians. Furthermore, one who could do this did not need to be paid for his service. The minister's motivation is God's love in Christ Jesus.

One pastor from Iowa Falls, Iowa, Rev. Ken Krueger, practices hospitality in the congregations he serves in order to get better acquainted with members and thereby enhance the ministry of the congregation. He invites approximately ten to fifteen members to one or two monthly sessions at his home. The agenda includes a devotion, often based upon John 1:12, and a message from Scripture that emphasizes that we are all brothers and sisters in Christ. As part of the same family, fellow Christians are encouraged to share a thumbnail sketch of their lives, their family, and other interesting biographical details. While the focus is on family relationships within the body, such an approach can't help but have a positive impact upon the total ministry of the church, including its outreach.

The same comments about the outreach dimension of 1 Timothy 3:2 apply to this verse. In the context of Titus 1, Paul also expresses a concern for those who oppose sound doctrine (1:9). There could be no such concern if the qualifications of a pastor were exclusively directed to the flock.

Hebrews 13:2

Do not forget to entertain strangers, for by so doing some people have entertained angels without knowing it. Hebrews 13:2

Among the five key verses, this verse is most clearly directed to the outsider, the stranger. The verse appears in a paragraph surrounded by admonitions on how to relate to fellow Christians, but the verse itself asks Christians to entertain strangers, not necessarily Christian strangers.

Perhaps you have heard some of the stories that are sometimes associated with this verse. The typical story goes something like this.

A Christian picks up a hitchhiker. Now this Christian ordinarily *never* picks up hitchhikers. He doesn't believe in doing this, because he thinks that one can never be too sure about whom you pick up. So when the Christian picks up this hitchhiker, you are led to believe that something *unusual* is in the air. The event takes place at night and it's raining, so perhaps the Christian felt sorry for the hitchhiker. The driver and hitchhiker engage in a conversation, find out that both of them are Christians, and the hitchhiker says that the Lord is coming soon. The hitchhiker asks the driver to go home a different way so as to drop him off at a better place on the way. The driver does so, and ten minutes later he hears on his car radio that the bridge he would have crossed by going home the normal way had been washed out by a flashflood that night. He probably never would have seen the problem in the dark and the rain and would have plunged to his death. When the driver turns to thank the hitchhiker, the hitchhiker is gone. Then the storyteller quotes this verse from Hebrews 13, "Do not forget to entertain strangers, for by so doing some people have entertained angels without knowing it."

Most versions of the story have one major problem. The problem is that no one knows just who the driver was, where this event took place, and what bridge had actually been washed out. I don't think the story is true. It's similar to the story about the lost day in time, alleged to be solved by the book of Joshua and a reference to the time of King Hezekiah. Later in this session I'll tell you what I think is the actual background to this verse in Hebrew 13.

Hebrews 13:2 begins with an imperative, a command. Receive both the brothers that we know and those we don't. Receive these traveling brothers. Give them lodging, food, information, and assistance. Remember that, for the most part, public hotels and lodging places were unknown at this time. In Genesis 18, Abraham received three men, washed their feet, butchered a fatted calf, and invited the men to eat with him. Later in that chapter the Lord spoke to Abraham about the destruction of Sodom and Gomorrah. Then, Genesis 19 begins, "The two angels arrived at Sodom in the evening." Nowhere in Genesis 18 are any of the visitors referred to as angels. The reader is left to surmise that one of the three visitors was the Lord in bodily form and the other two were the angels who are mentioned in chapter 19.

In Genesis 19, Lot also entertained angels unawares when he invited two of them into his home and prepared a meal for them. Lenski, commenting on Hebrews 13:2, states, "The thought of the statement can hardly be that by entertaining strangers we, too, may have the good fortune of sometimes receiving angels into our homes... . It is sufficient to say that, as some were unexpectedly blessed by receiving strangers, so we, too, may be thus blessed."[13] Hospitality to strangers ranked high as a virtue; it was indeed, a religious obligation.

1 Peter 4:9

Offer hospitality to one another without grumbling.
1 Peter 4:9

Verse eight is an introduction to this verse and an explanation of the attitude with which one offers hospitality: "Above all, love each other deeply, because love covers over a multitude of sins" (1 Peter 4:8). Love each other, and then love the stranger. 1 Peter 4:9 itself is often read against the backdrop of the other verses already discussed. According to Bigg in his commentary on 1 Peter, this verse has to do with "the reception, entertainment, and relief of travellers. Inns were rare and little used, though we read of them in two passages of St. Luke's Gospel, ii. 7 (Mary & Joseph), x. 34 (the Good Samaritan). The entertainment of strangers was specially enjoined by our Lord (Matt[hew] xxv. 35, 'I was a stranger and you invited me in')."[14] Some new Christians lost friends by becoming Christians, so the need for hospitality was more urgent. Hospitality was to be offered without resentment or complaining; it was a Christian privilege.

Lenski in his interpretation of 1 Peter states, "Even pagans remarked about how the Christians loved each other and received a wholly strange Christian as a brother."[15] As Jesus said, "A new command I give you: Love one another. As I have loved you, so you must love one another. By this all men will know that you are My disciples, if you love one another" (John 13:34–35). In other words, love them until they ask you why. While the poorest should also do so, those with means should be first to offer hospitality "without grumbling" (1 Peter 4:9).

1 Peter 4:9 also contains an important reciprocal idea in the use of the words "one another." Christians should both extend hospitality and receive hospitality. Note, for example, Acts 16:15 and 16:40, where Paul and his companions benefited from the hospitality of Lydia. In Philemon 22, Paul asked Philemon to prepare a guestroom for him, that he might benefit from Philemon's hospitality. This, then, is one of the purposes of hosting traveling Christians, since many of those traveling Christians, like Paul, were missionaries. Certainly the offering of hospitality to the missionary was an aid to the spread of the Gospel. Could it not also be used today to aid the spread of the Gospel in another way, even if the dominant reason for such hospitality in the first-century world was to aid other believers?

The primary focus of 1 Peter 4:9 is the activity of believers. After all, those are the people to whom this epistle is addressed. However, we must remember that this book contains numerous references to the importance of Christian witnessing. This is the Epistle of Suffering that contains advice for Christians on how to live in trying circumstances. It gives advice to wives on how to relate to their husbands, "so that, if any of them do not believe the word, they may be won over without words by the behavior of their wives" (1 Peter 3:1). Another familiar verse is 1 Peter 3:15: "But in your hearts set apart Christ as Lord. Always be prepared to give an answer to everyone who asks you to give the reason for the hope that you have." Elsewhere Peter is concerned about the impact of our lives upon the unbelieving world (1 Peter 2:12; 4:12–19). Within the concern of this epistle for the witness of the Christian, the practice of hospitality may well be intended to benefit both the believer and the unbeliever and therefore should not be limited to hospitality for the traveler.

To read 1 Peter 4:9 as though it had only to do with receiving travelers is to read too much into the verse. The general nature of the verse admits to a much broader interpretation without denying its application to travelers in the New Testament world.

Summary of the Five Key Passages

In summary, then, what do these five passages tell us?

1. Hospitality is one of the most important Christian privileges.
2. Hospitality is motivated by love.
3. Practice hospitality freely, without coercion and without grumbling—hospitality motivated by love.
4. Christians motivated by the Holy Spirit practice hospitality toward one another.
5. Fellowship is practiced among Christians only, while hospitality may be practiced toward Christian and non-Christian.
6. Pastors especially need to practice hospitality.
7. There is no suggestion that hospitality should not be exercised for Christian outreach, and there are some hints that this should occur.
8. Christians are willing to be either the giver or the recipient of hospitality.
9. Hospitality should be actively pursued or practiced. Don't fall into hospitality; plan for it.
10. Hospitality does not mean simply to entertain and to feast with friends but also to take in Christian strangers or acquaintances when these are traveling or when they are fleeing from persecutions.
11. Hospitality is not a distinctively New Testament practice nor a distinctively Jewish or Christian practice. It was practiced in the Old and New Testaments, among Christians and non-Christians, and by Jews and Gentiles in ancient times.

Hospitality in the New Testament

In addition to the five occurrences of a form of the primary word for hospitality, there are five other words that appear in the New Testament. The word *xenizo,* "to recèive as a guest, entertain," occurs ten times. The word *xenia,* "hospitality, entertainment, guest room," occurs twice. The word *xenodocheo,* "to show hospitality," occurs once. The word *xenos,* "stranger," "host," occurs fourteen times. The word *hypolambano,* "to receive as a guest, support," occurs once in the sense of being hospitable.

In summary, then, the New Testament has thirty-three passages that contain one of seven different words related to the concept of hospitality, and six of the seven contain some form of the word for stranger. The concept of hospitality is a common one in the New Testament. And, as we will see, the Old Testament also contains numerous examples of the practice of hospitality.

The seven occurrences of the English words *hospitality* or *hospitable* in the New International Version translate four of the words listed immediately above or discussed earlier:

1. "Share with God's people who are in need. *Practice hospitality*" (Romans 12:13, one of the five key passages).
2. "Gaius, whose *hospitality* [he is the *xenos,* "stranger," only here in the New Testament in the sense of a host] I and the whole church here enjoy, sends you his greetings" (Romans 16:23).
3. "… and is well known for her good deeds, such as bringing up children, *showing hospitality* [*xenodocheo*], washing the feet of the saints, helping those in trouble and devoting herself to all kinds of good deeds" (1 Timothy 5:10).
4. "*Offer hospitality* to one another without grumbling" (1 Peter 4:9, another of the five key passages).
5. "We ought therefore to *show hospitality* [*hypolambano,* "to receive as a guest, support," literally "to take up," only here with this meaning in the New Testament] to such men so that we may work together for the truth" (3 John 8).
6. "Now the overseer must be above reproach, the husband of but one wife, temperate, self-controlled, respectable, *hospitable,* able to teach" (1 Timothy 3:2, one of the five key passages).
7. "Rather he must be *hospitable,* one who loves what is good, who is self-controlled, upright, holy and disciplined" (Titus 1:8, another of the five key passages.)

Outside of these passages, however, there are also numerous references to the concept of hospitality in the New Testament, some of which are included in the paragraphs that follow. The reader will note far more frequent references to hospitality in the narrative sections of the New Testament, such as the Gospels and the Book of Acts, for there the culture of the first century A.D. is more easily observed. We see just how people lived their lives. The Pauline epistles, however, speak to those issues that the apostle felt needed addressing, far less often showing the significance of hospitality in that culture. Since hospitality was so much a given, problems in this area rarely occurred and therefore did not need Paul's advice.

The Gospels, especially the Gospel of Luke with its concern for inclusion, contain references to hospitality. The innkeeper provided the holy family with a place to stay, even though there was no room for them (Luke 2:7). The calling of Levi demonstrates hospitality, for Jesus welcomes Levi into the circle of disciples. On this occasion, Levi, or Matthew, held a banquet for Jesus and invited fellow tax collectors to the banquet (Matthew 9:9–13; Mark 2:13–17; Luke 5:27–32). So Levi is both the giver of hospitality, for he hosted the banquet, and the recipient of hospitality, since Jesus, the perfect host, welcomed him as a disciple.

Herod Antipas had many traits we do not admire, but he was a hospitable host at least once, including a meal on the occasion (Matthew 14:1–12; Mark 6:14–29; Luke 9:7–9). The Parable of the Unjust Servant illustrates that servant's concern for being welcomed into the homes of those he served before losing his job (Luke 16:4). The master commended him, and Jesus told his audience that they should use worldly wealth to gain friends "so that when it is gone, you will be welcomed into eternal dwellings" (Luke 16:9). The Lord's Supper was instituted in someone's home (Matthew 26:18; Mark 14:14; Luke 22:10–11). The trial of Jesus took place, in part, at the home of Caiaphas (Matthew 26:57–68; Mark 14:53–65; Luke 22:63–71), undoubtedly, in part, because of the willingness of Caiaphas to open his home to colleagues. On at least one occasion, the resurrection was announced to the disciples in someone's house (John 20:26). But many of the references to hospitality in the Gospels will be discussed in the next session.

In the Book of Acts, Pentecost began while the disciples were gathered in a house (Acts 2:2). The Gospel was proclaimed both in the temple courts and in people's homes, perhaps around the hospitality of the host (Acts 5:42). That Christians might enjoy the hospitality of unbelievers was a new idea for the fledgling Christian church, one that it did not swallow easily.

Shortly after Jesus appeared to Paul on the road to Damascus, Paul benefited from the hospitality of Judas (Acts 9:11). At that house Ananias laid hands on Paul that he might see (Acts 9:17). Peter stayed at the home of Simon the Tanner (Acts 9:43; 10:6) and went to the house of Mary, John Mark's mother (Acts 12:12). Peter was also aware of the significance of the home as a place to preach the word of the Lord, for he invited the visitors from Cornelius to spend the night (Acts 10:23) and Cornelius heard the Gospel preached by Peter himself in Cornelius' own home (Acts 10:22, 25).

In Philippi, Paul and his companions benefited from the hospitality of Lydia, who, with her household, was baptized. She said, "If you consider me a believer in the Lord, ... come and stay at my house" (Acts 16:15). In the same chapter, Paul and Silas spoke the word of the Lord to the jailer "and to all the others in his house" and spent some time in the jailer's house with his family, all of whom had believed (Acts 16:32, 34).

In Acts 17, while Paul and Silas were in Thessalonica, Paul spoke in the synagogue for three consecutive Sabbaths, teaching that Jesus was the Messiah. They apparently stayed at the home of Jason, since the Jews came to Jason's house in search of Paul and Silas, saying that "Jason has welcomed them into his house" (Acts 17:5, 7). In this case, as in other cases, Paul the veteran believer benefited from a new believer.

In Corinth, Paul enjoyed the hospitality of Priscilla and Aquila, actually living in their home. Luke writes, "because he [Paul] was a tentmaker as they were, he stayed and worked with them" (Acts 18:3). In Acts 18:7, we note that in Corinth, when he was no longer welcome in the synagogue, "Paul left the synagogue and went next door to the house of Titius Justus, a worshiper of God." There many of the Corinthians heard Paul speak and believed. Priscilla and Aquila, two people who obviously were quite hospitable, also received Apollos, and when Apollos went from Ephesus to Corinth they provided him with a letter urging that he be received there (Acts 18:26–27).

Paul tells the Ephesian elders, "You know that I have not hesitated to preach anything that would be helpful to you but have taught you publicly and from house to house" (Acts 20:20). Clearly Paul used both public places and the homes of people for the proclamation of the Gospel and the teaching of the Word of God. Later, on his trip to Jerusalem, he benefited from the hospitality of Philip the evangelist at Caesarea (Acts 21:8) and from the hospitality of Mnason, one of the early disciples, in Jerusalem (Acts 21:16).

Donald Wayne Riddle notes that "in the story of Paul's painful way to Rome it is mentioned that the pagan, Publius, courteously entertained the party for three days."[16] Luke says that they were the guests of Publius (Acts 28:7). With "unusual kindness" the people of Malta received the shipwrecked contingency that included Paul (Acts 28:1–2). Christians are not the only ones who practice hospitality. But Paul, who so often benefited from the hospitality of others, especially Christians, also practiced hospitality himself, as we read in Acts 28:30: "For two whole years Paul stayed there in his own rented house and welcomed all who came to see him."

In the epistles, we note the endings of various epistles (e.g., 3 John, with its mutual salutations of friends), although friendship is not necessarily an indication of hospitality. The ending of the book of Romans offers similar insight. Although he had not previously visited Rome, Paul expected to benefit from the hospitality of the Romans, as Romans 15:24 and the reference to Gaius as host in 16:23 indicate.

3 John 10 speaks against the practice of not welcoming a brother. And 2 John 10–11 urges Christians to refuse hospitality to someone who is a false teacher. 3 John speaks in verse 5 of helping fellow Christians even though they are strangers and uses one of the related hospitality words in verse 8, when John says that "we ought therefore to show hospitality to such men."

In Philemon 22, Paul asked Philemon to prepare a guest room for him, that he might benefit from Philemon's hospitality. While he had visited the Corinthians, he clearly expected to enjoy their hospitality in the future (1 Corinthians 16:5–9; 2 Corinthians 1:15; 2:1–3). When he commended Titus to the Corinthians (2 Corinthians 7:15), he no doubt expected that they would be hospitable toward this traveling missionary. In Galatians 1:18, Paul writes about his visit to Jerusalem "to get acquainted with Peter," stating that he "stayed with him fifteen days," obviously benefiting from the hospitality of Peter. In Galatians 6:2, Paul enjoins, "Carry each other's burdens, and in this way you will fulfill the law of Christ." That could easily include the practice of hospitality. In Philippians 2:29, Paul asks the Philippians to welcome Epaphroditus when he comes. He speaks similarly for Mark when he writes to the Colossians (4:10) and for Onesimus in his letter to Philemon (v. 17). Paul stated that people should be told about the good things widows have done, among them being hospitable (1 Timothy 5:10).

Hospitality in the Old Testament

In the Old Testament, hospitality is likewise based upon love of the stranger. Examples of love in the sense of *phileo,* friendship, appear, and examples of hospitality are common. David's friendship with Jonathan is perhaps the finest example of love between two people in the entire Old Testament (1 Samuel 18:1, 3; 19:1; 20:17). The friendship between God and the patriarchs, Abraham, Isaac, and Jacob, is the model. God is the initiator in many such relationships. God is the host, and the befriended people are His guests in this world. But friendship alone is not evidence of hospitality.

When the writer to the Hebrews commands us, "Do not forget to entertain strangers" (13:20), Abraham's experience in Genesis 18, and perhaps Lot's experience in Genesis 19, was probably in his mind. Abraham entertained three visitors. Genesis 18:2 describes them as "three men." As they were leaving, the Lord spoke with Abraham about the destruction of Sodom and Gomorrah. In the next chapter two angels went to Sodom to meet Lot. Apparently the "three men" were the Lord and two angels, appearing in human form. In the opening verses of Genesis 19, Lot extended hospitality to the angels, providing a place for them to wash their feet, to eat a meal, and to spend the night (Genesis 19:1–4). Therefore, both Abraham and Lot entertained angels without knowing it.

Near the end of his search for a wife for Isaac, Abraham's chief servant enjoyed the hospitality of Rebekah and her brother, Laban, who welcomed him into their home, served him a meal, and provided for his men and his camels (Genesis 24:25, 31–32, 54). They even provided water "for him and his men to wash their feet" (Genesis 24:32), that ancient indication of hospitality. Not many years later, Jacob benefited from the hospitality of God at Bethel (Genesis 28:10–22), a place name that means literally "the house of God," and then from the hospitality of Laban (Genesis 29:13–14). Jacob and his family left Paddan Aram when they no longer felt they enjoyed the hospitality of Laban (Genesis 31:14–16).

Moses was a guest in the house of Jethro, or Reuel (Exodus 2:20–21), hundreds of years after the pharaoh of Egypt had extended the hospitality of the land to the family of Joseph (Genesis 47:5–6). Later Moses married one of Reuel's daughters. Reuel, apparently accustomed to being hospitable, scolded his daughters, "Why did you leave him? Invite him to have something to eat" (Exodus 2:20). Some time later Moses was able to return the favor to his father-in-law (Exodus 18:7). Indeed, the Books of Exodus, Numbers, and Deuteronomy record the wandering of the homeless Israelite people in the Sinai desert and the blessings of a hospitable God, who befriended them at Marah and Elim (Exodus 15:22–27) and other places and who welcomed them into his family at Sinai (Exodus 19). This same God provided food for them in the provision of manna at a time when food was difficult to come by (Exodus 16). In the same narrative, God records the inhospitable character of Edom (Numbers 20:14–21) and the Amorites (Numbers 21:22–23), who would not allow Israel to pass through their territory.

In Deuteronomy 10:12–19, Moses wrote about the approach the Israelites were to take when they came to the Promised Land. "And you are to love those who are aliens, for you yourselves were aliens in Egypt" (10:19). Those who know what it feels like to be strangers most readily befriend those who actually are strangers. All Christians, in one sense, know the feeling of alienation because of sin, and we know the welcome that God gives through Jesus Christ and His forgiveness. Knowing that, we can welcome others into the Christian church and the family of God.

Just prior to the conquest of Canaan, two spies benefited in an unusual manner from the hospitality of a prostitute by the name of Rahab (Joshua 2:1). Later, Israel returned the favor and welcomed Rahab and her family into the family of Israel (Joshua 6:23, 25). After the crossing of the Jordan, God welcomed the Israelites into their new home by providing food for them through the land, thereby obviating the need for manna (Joshua 5:11–12). In their new land, the Israelites were to live in peace and according to the Word and will of God, treating the aliens among them like those who were native born (Leviticus 19:34).

F. F. Bruce concludes that the writer to the Hebrews, writing in Hebrews 13:2, may also have had in mind those angels who appeared to Gideon (Judges 6:11–24), Manoah and his wife (Judges 13:3–23), and Tobit (Tobit 3:17; 5:4–5, where the angel Raphael visits Tobias, "but Tobias did not know it"). Bruce says that some of your visitors "will prove to be true messengers of God to [you], bringing a greater blessing than they receive."[17]

In spite of his oppression, Eglon extended hospitality to Ehud, a hospitality that made his undoing possible (Judges 3:19–21). In spite of her treachery, Jael extended the customary hospitality to Sisera, the Canaanite general whom Barak defeated in battle near Mount Tabor (Judges 4:17–20). When the Levite from the hill country of Ephraim was returning home after a stay in Bethlehem, he stopped in the town of Gibeah. When an old man, also originally from the hill country of Ephraim but now living in Gibeah, saw him, he said, "You are welcome at my house... . Let me supply whatever you need" (Judges 19:20).

Nabal's refusal to extend hospitality to David and his men almost resulted in the death of every male in his company and indirectly resulted in his own death (1 Samuel 25). Nathan's rebuke of David is based on a story that presupposes hospitality (2 Samuel 12:1–4). The rich man would never have taken the little ewe lamb from his neighbor if a traveler had not come to visit him. Solomon's building of the temple provided the nation with the opportunity to extend the hospitality of God to the nation and to many Gentiles who would come to Jerusalem (1 Kings 6; 2 Chronicles 6:32–33). When the Queen of Sheba visited Solomon, he entertained her (1 Kings 10).

Elijah enjoyed the hospitality of the widow at Zarephath, and she greatly benefited herself (1 Kings 17:9–16). When Elijah could no longer count on the tolerance of Ahab and Jezebel, he threw himself upon the hospitality of God at the mountain of God and there received encouragement for the task (1 Kings 19). What a lesson we could learn from that story! Elisha was hospitably received by the Shunammite woman (2 Kings 4), "who urged him to stay for a meal" (4:8) and provided a room for him to stay (4:10).

The Books of Ezra and Nehemiah testify to the desire of God's people to return to their homeland, while Esther is a testimony to the desire to protect those Jews who no longer live in their own homeland.

Job must have been a hospitable man, for he spent seven days at his home with his three friends, Eliphaz, Bildad, and Zophar, before they spoke to him (Job 2:11–13). In one of Job's speeches

34

of self-defense, he spoke of his own practice of hospitality: "But no stranger had to spend the night in the street, for my door was always open to the traveler" (Job 31:32).

This look at the Scriptures shows that both the Old Testament and the New Testament testify frequently to the importance of hospitality for individuals, families, and nations. But there is more to the New Testament picture of hospitality, especially in the life of Jesus, and to that we now turn our attention.

Discussion

1. Among the people you know, who seems especially good at opening their home to other people? What is it about them that makes them so hospitable? When you are in their home, what do you notice about their home, their attitude, their behavior?

2. What places are known for their hospitality? What restaurants? What other localities? Are they more hospitable than your church? Ought that to be the case?

3. What different houses are mentioned in the following verses? What relationship exists between them?
   Genesis 28:17, 19

   Luke 2:16

   Luke 19:47

John 14:2

2 Corinthians 6:16

4. How does Jesus react in John 2:16? In Luke 19:45–46?

5. What stereotypes did David break, according to Jesus? See Matthew 12:4; cf. also Mark 2:26; Luke 6:4.

6. How could David do something reserved only for priests?

7. What can we do to practice hospitality in our church? How might it benefit our ministry?

8. How does the Christmas story illustrate the importance of hospitality from the beginning of Jesus' life? See Luke 2:7. The calling of Levi also demonstrates hospitality (Luke 5:27–32). In what ways is hospitality demonstrated? Why?

9. How did Paul benefit from the practice of hospitality in Acts 9:11, 17? How did Peter benefit from the practice of hospitality in Acts 9:43, 10:6, 23? In Acts 2:2, what event took place in someone's house? Why is this significant?

Endnotes

1. C. S. Lewis, *The Four Loves* (Glasgow: HarperCollins, 1977), 33.
2. The quotes from the *Theological Dictionary of the New Testament* in this book are from the article on *phileo* and *philos* by Gustav Stählin (Grand Rapids: Eerdmans, 1974).
3. *Fellowship Evangelism* is the title of a package of articles from *Net Results*, a publication devoted to the evangelistic task of the church. However, I don't mean to pick on *Net Results*. The issue is not terminology but the effective proclamation of the Gospel by the Christian church.
4. William Sanday and Arthur C. Headlam, *A Critical and Exegetical Commentary on the Epistle to the Romans,* 5th ed. (Edinburgh: T. & T. Clark), 362–63.
5. Martin H. Franzmann, *Romans,* Concordia Commentary (St. Louis: Concordia, 1968), 226–27.
6. R. C. H. Lenski, *The Interpretation of St. Paul's Epistle to the Romans* (1936; reprint, Minneapolis: Augsburg, 1961), 772.
7. Thomas D. Lea and Hayne P. Griffin Jr., *1, 2 Timothy, Titus,* New American Commentary (Nashville: Broadman, 1992), 110.
8. R. C. H. Lenski, *The Interpretation of St. Paul's Epistles to the Colossians, to the Thessalonians, to Timothy, to Titus and to Philemon* (1937; reprint, Minneapolis: Augsburg, 1961), 583.
9. Donald Wayne Riddle, "Early Christian Hospitality: A Factor in the Gospel Transmission," *Journal of Biblical Literature* 57 (1938): 149.
10. Joseph Aldrich, *Lifestyle Evangelism: Learning to Open Your Life to Those Around You* (Sisters, Oreg.: Questar Publishers), 139.
11. Lea and Griffin, *1, 2 Timothy, Titus,* 284; emphasis added.
12. Lea and Griffin, *1, 2 Timothy, Titus,* 284, citing J. N. D. Kelly, *The Pastoral Epistles.*
13. R. C. H. Lenski, *The Interpretation of the Epistle to the Hebrews and the Epistle of James* (Minneapolis: Augsburg, 1966), 469.
14. Charles Bigg, *A Critical and Exegetical Commentary on the Epistles of St. Peter and St. Jude,* International Critical Commentary 42 (Edinburgh: T. & T. Clark, 1961), 173.

15. R. C. H. Lenski, *The Interpretation of the Epistles of St. Peter, St. John and St. Jude* (Minneapolis: Augsburg, 1966), 196.
16. Riddle, "Early Christian Hospitality," 152.
17. F. F. Bruce, *The Epistle to the Hebrews*. New International Commentary on the New Testament (Grand Rapids: Eerdmans, 1964), 389–91.

Session 3 Hospitality in the Life of Jesus

*M*ankind is broken loose from moral band; No rights of
hospitality remain. Ovid, *Metamorphoses*

Jesus once said, "Foxes have holes and birds of the air have nests, but the Son of Man has no place to lay His head" (Matthew 8:20; Luke 9:58). Jesus never owned a home, and He did not therefore have the ability to invite others into that home, except that He could invite people to the home where He was staying (see, for example, John 1:39). When He died, He was buried in a borrowed tomb. So how we can write about hospitality in the life of Jesus? We can do so because Jesus is the great host. He has created a home in which people might live (this world), and He offers another perfect home to which believers will one day go (heaven), as 2 Peter 1:11 declares: "You will receive a *rich welcome* into the eternal kingdom of our Lord and Savior Jesus Christ." He made that possible by Himself coming to us in human form (Philippians 2:6–7) and making Himself at home with our human nature and therefore at home with us (John 1:14), by paying the penalty for our sin by His death on the cross, and by rising from the dead, thus defeating our great enemy death.

Having become one of us in the incarnation, Jesus made use of the culture of His day, a culture that highly prized hospitality. Jesus tells us, "In My Father's house are many rooms.... . I am going there to prepare a place for you" (John 14:2). By these words, Jesus promises us a place in the Father's house; He assures us that we will be the recipients of His and His Father's hospitality. One day, Jesus teaches, "The owner of the house will come back" (Mark 13:35). He bids us to be ready.

In the meantime, we are guests in His home by virtue of being a part of His creation. We are also guests in His special family, the body of Christ, by His grace. We who are guests of God, who have been "called by the Gospel" and "enlightened with His gifts" (Small Catechism), demonstrate our appreciation for His grace by serving as hosts to others who are as yet outside of God's special family. No one was better at using the hospitable setting of the home for ministry than Jesus, in spite of the fact that He was most often the recipient of the hospitality rather than the giver of hospitality.

This session will illustrate Jesus as the great host during His ministry by looking at various accounts in the Gospels. As the great host, Jesus enjoys the houses of others, but especially the house of His Father: "Didn't you know I had to be in My Father's house?" (Luke 2:49).

Furthermore, notice that Jesus, the great host, who has created a home for us both in this world and the next, shapes His people into a house themselves. Peter writes, "You also, like living stones, are being built into *a spiritual house* to be a holy priesthood, offering spiritual sacrifices acceptable to God through Jesus Christ" (1 Peter 2:5). But that is the sense in which we enjoy God's blessings in this life, for the church is not a building, but a gathering of people who have been redeemed by Christ.

A Key Text: Luke 14:12–14

When we think about Jesus, hospitality, and evangelism, we start in Luke 14:12–14. According to the *Theological Dictionary of the New Testament* (9:160; Eerdmans), "the wall of the exclusiveness of fellowship and love which is at issue here, and of which all groups at all times have been guilty, is what Jesus is trying to break down in His community." Luke 14:12–14 shows that friendship and table fellowship are partners. In his commentary on Luke, William Arndt entitles his discussion of these verses "Unselfish Hospitality."[1] Here Jesus enjoys the hospitality of another and uses the occasion to teach a lesson on reaching out to others. Luke writes:

> Then Jesus said to his host, "When you give a luncheon or dinner, do not invite your friends, your brothers or relatives, or your rich neighbors; if you do, they may invite you back and so you will be repaid. But when you give a banquet, invite the poor, the crippled, the lame, the blind, and you will be blessed. Although they cannot repay you, you will be repaid at the resurrection of the righteous."

Here Jesus taught His host, a prominent Pharisee (Luke 14:1), who apparently invited friends, relatives, and rich neighbors, that he should invite those who cannot pay him back. That would be the essence of love and unselfishness and result in blessing for the host. This is, of course, true and demonstrates the importance of hospitality. Jesus Himself entered the house of a Gentile when He visited Tyre (Mark 7:24) and commended a Gentile woman from Zarephath (Luke 4:26), both outcasts in the eyes of the Jews and examples of the type of people Jesus wanted the Pharisee to invite.

However, we cannot invite just the physically poor, crippled, lame, and blind, but also those who are spiritually poor and crippled. In inviting these people, we have opportunity to share "not only the gospel of God but our lives as well" (1 Thessalonians 2:8).

This hospitable lifestyle must flow out of the believer's love for Jesus. In John's Gospel, for example, Jesus demands the unconditional love of His disciples and a readiness for total commitment. In John 21:15–17, the threefold questioning ("Do you truly love me more than these?" and so on) and the threefold affirmation ("Yes, Lord" and so on) are made clear by the threefold commission ("Feed My lambs"; "Take care of My sheep"; "Feed My sheep"). This suggests the lifestyle Jesus wants His disciples to live and empowers them to live as they carry on after the resurrection and ascension. It was a lifestyle that would include both the expression of hospitality and benefiting from the hospitality of others.

In His Preaching and Teaching

Opportunities to teach the Word of God to non-Christians today are rather rare. Most non-Christians will not enter a church voluntarily, but they will enter a Christian's home. In that relaxed atmosphere, they can ask questions and find answers. They can assess the sincerity of the people they meet, evaluate the credibility of the things they hear, and rethink the wisdom of the prejudices they hold. They can talk openly without fear of retaliation or ridicule. They can express their ideas, and they most often listen to the ideas of others when they find that their own ideas are heard. This is the value of the home Bible study in today's world, something akin to the teaching of Jesus in the home. Jesus is present in the home Bible study today, just as He was present in the homes of many of the people with whom He came in contact during His lifetime.

According to Edith Schaeffer, Matthew 25:35–40 is "an underlying base for it all."[2] Along with Luke 14:12–14, this teaching of Jesus is one of the fundamental sections of Scripture expressing the importance of showing hospitality. In showing hospitality to others, we are showing hospitality to Christ Himself. We do so, not merely in our inviting of the stranger, but also in meeting the needs of food and drink, clothing and companionship, caring and comfort. Jesus teaches in that passage:

> "For I was hungry and you gave Me something to eat, I was thirsty and you gave Me something to drink, *I was a stranger and you invited Me in,* I needed clothes and you clothed Me, I was sick and you looked after Me, I was in prison and you came to visit Me."
>
> Then the righteous will answer Him, "Lord, when did we see You hungry and feed You, or thirsty and give You something to drink? When did we see You a stranger and invite You in, or needing clothes and clothe You? When did we see You sick or in prison and go to visit You?"
>
> The King will reply, "I tell you the truth, whatever you did for one of the least of these brothers of Mine, you did for Me."

Parables

The parables of Jesus especially include numerous examples of the importance of hospitality, and Jesus seemed to single out the importance of hospitality to the unlikely, the undeserving, and the undesirable. Consider, for example, the Parable of the Prodigal (Luke 15:11–32) and the elder brother, who at once thought of his friends when he saw the feast for his brother. The fortunate finders of Luke 15:6, 9 (lost sheep, lost coin) summoned their friends to a feast, where they rejoiced with those who are a part of their circle of family and friends. Jesus was one for whom family and friends were important, and the gathering of people into these groups of utmost concern. The experience of being hospitable or benefiting from the hospitality of others was common not only in Jesus' life but also in His teaching.

Jesus also taught the Parable of the Unjust Steward, whose master found the steward arranging things so that "people [would] welcome [him] into their houses" (Luke 16:4) after he left his job. In another parable, Jesus told about the rich man who ignored Lazarus and was guilty of a lack of hospitality toward the beggar who lay at his gate (Luke 16:20–21).

In the parable in Luke 11:5–8, a friend asked for bread for visitors from one who was in bed. This parable implies that a true friend does not hesitate to meet the requests of a friend (i.e., to be hospitable). If that is the case, Jesus taught, how much more prompt will God be to meet our requests? Indeed, that is the point of the context, for Luke goes on to record the words of Jesus, "Ask and it will be given to you; seek and you will find; knock and the door will be opened to you" (Luke 11:9).

Even the Parable of the Good Samaritan hints at the value of hospitality. Had that Samaritan been able to bring the half-dead traveler into his own home, he would undoubtedly have done so. After all, he bandaged his wounds, took him to an inn, covered the expense, and looked in on him again later (Luke 10:25–35). Being unable to bring the traveler into his own home, he did the next best thing.

Other Teachings

Jesus also taught about hospitality without using parables. For example, Luke records the story of a dinner party to which Jesus was invited, where a woman washed Jesus' feet. The party took place at the home of a Pharisee, who may have been more concerned about rubbing shoulders with this popular, new Jewish teacher than with showing this teacher the customary hospitality. After all, he didn't put oil on Jesus' head nor provide water for Jesus' feet. But Jesus used the setting to teach about the forgiveness of sins (Luke 7:36–50).

Jesus taught that friendship is closely related to service (for example, the friends of the centurion, Luke 7:6, are at his service), concern, and sacrifice. Friendship results in serving the one in need, being concerned about his or her welfare, and making a sacrifice at a time of day when few people wish to be bothered. Friendship toward the stranger is remarkable in that one expects friends to care for you; one doesn't expect this of strangers. And strangers notice. Those concepts of friendship toward insider, outsider, and outcast, service toward those in need, and sacrifice saturate the teaching of Jesus and reflect an undercurrent of hospitality that is seldom met in today's world.

Friendship doesn't always result in hospitality, nor are Christians always ready to provide hospitality to the stranger. Sin is always ready to raise its ugly head. Therefore, in His teaching, Jesus gave warnings about unreliable friends in Luke 21:16–17, where the love for parents, children, and brothers is reversed and friends are changed into enemies. Jesus was visiting inside a house (Mark 3:20) at a time when He was accused of being possessed by Beelzebub, so He subsequently taught about the problem of a divided kingdom. Those we most expect to be hospitable toward us may end up being inhospitable. Those who rejected Jesus would find their house desolate (Matthew 23:38) and themselves unable to render hospitality to anyone. But clearly, Jesus teaches the importance of hospitality toward the stranger.

In His Miracles

While not all of Jesus' miracles were done in people's homes, the fact that many of them were done in that context suggests still further the importance of the home to Jesus. He recognized the importance of the home to those who were sick, and He would undoubtedly, for example, approve of the hospice movement today and the desire of some terminally ill people to return home for their last hours. He would endorse the movement toward a more comfortable, friendlier, and more homelike room for the hospital patient.

Jesus' first miracle took place at a wedding, probably held in the home of the bridegroom (John 2:1–11). Jesus healed the mother-in-law of Peter in Simon Peter's home, and it was from that same home that He healed "all the sick and demon-possessed" (Matthew 8:14–16; Mark 1:29–34; Luke 4:38–41). Mark explicitly states that "the whole town gathered at the door, and Jesus healed many who had various diseases" (Mark 1:33–34).

At the time of the healing of the paralytic, Mark tells us that Jesus had just come home to Capernaum (Mark 2:1–12). People packed the house to hear Him, and four men especially worked hard to bring a friend into the presence of Jesus. After Jesus healed the man, He sent the man to *his* home (Matthew 9:6–7). When Jesus healed the daughter of Jairus, a ruler of the synagogue, that took place in a house (Mark 5:35–43). Notice also, however, that Jesus put the crowd outside of the house in recognition of their unbelief at His words. The home is to be a place where faith is nurtured, not a place where unbelief is encouraged.

When Jesus offered to heal the servant of a Roman army officer from Capernaum, He was willing to come to the officer's home

(Matthew 8:7–8). Jesus healed two blind men in someone's home (Matthew 9:27–31). Jesus healed in the synagogue (Matthew 12:9–13) and in the temple area (Matthew 21:14). The temple was the home of Jesus in the sense that it was God's house.

After Jesus healed the demon-possessed man, recognizing that the home was the place where that man's witness would be most effective, Jesus sent the man home, saying, "Go home to your family and tell them how much the Lord has done for you" (Mark 5:19).

Even the miracles of the feeding of the five thousand (Matthew 14:13–21; Mark 6:30–44; Luke 9:10–17; John 6:1–14) and the four thousand (Matthew 15:29–39; Mark 8:1–10) are times when Jesus entertained others with His miraculous powers and His captivating words. He entertained them in the sense that He was the host, not in the sense that He performed for them. As will be stated later, Jesus simply did what a host would do—He fed His guests and taught them.

In His Sharing of Meals

American Christians need to learn again the importance of sharing meals with our neighbors, whether Christian or non-Christian. We have too often fallen prey to the "eat and run" mentality. A friend recently observed that while attending college, she noticed that Americans eat quickly and depart. International students, however, turn the meal into an event and take the time to converse. Many Americans do this as well, but far too many Americans eat quickly so they can get on with life. Perhaps we have visited too many fast-food restaurants to realize the importance of the communication that needs to take place, especially in the family, at meal times. Too many people are running in too many directions at once, even within the same family. We need to slow down, smell the roses, take it easy, kick off the shoes, and get reacquainted. We need to make mealtime an important family event as well as a potential Christian outreach.

Talk to a restaurant owner or employee and discover that person's perspective on hospitality. One individual told me that she was in the hospitality business. I asked her what that meant, and she told me that she owned a restaurant. If customers don't feel welcome or if the atmosphere is not inviting, they are unlikely to return. Then the restaurant is out of business. The same is true of some friends who own a ranch in Valley Park, Missouri. People won't come out to ride their horses if they aren't received well when they come. If more businesses saw themselves as being in the hospitality business, fewer businesses would fail.

The well-known television sitcom *Cheers* portrayed a place of hospitality, as the regulars yelled, "Norm," whenever Norm appeared on the scene. Everyone felt at home, even in the midst of life's ups and downs. When a bar is a place "where everybody knows your name" and a church is not, then, I submit, something is wrong. Perhaps we in the church can learn something from the bars of this world about the needs of people for meaningful relationships. Where else ought people to be able to feel especially welcome than in the Christian church? If more Christians acted as hospitably as Norm's friends in *Cheers,* this book would be unnecessary.

The passage with which this session opened (Luke 14:12–14) was a meal at the home of a Pharisee. There Jesus taught the Pharisees about pride and humility, so that passage could just as easily have been included in the section "In His Preaching and Teaching." Beyond that example, there are many other instances where Jesus shared a meal with the people around Him. Some of those people were His followers, such as Mary and Martha, and many were not.

The House of Mary and Martha

The familiar story of Mary listening to Jesus while Martha prepared the meal is set against the background of hospitality, for "Martha opened her home to Him" (Luke 10:38–42, especially 10:38). Perhaps we have judged Martha too harshly for her unwillingness to listen to Jesus, especially since it is the first mention of Martha in the Gospels. She may not have met Jesus prior to this event. Certainly she deserved the rebuke she received, but who among us has ever commended her for her hospitality? After all, Luke mentions "all the preparations that had to be made" (10:40), not disputing that fact. He only notes that she was distracted by those preparations to the point of ignoring the teaching of Jesus.

The House of Simon the Leper

In John 12:1–8 (Matthew 26:6–13 and Mark 14:3–9 are parallel passages), we read that Jesus arrived at Bethany. "Here a dinner was given in Jesus' honor" (John 12:2). Then Mary anointed the feet of Jesus with a pint of expensive perfume, a sign of her great love displayed within the exercise of hospitality. Jesus was one of those people whom others loved to invite to dinner.

The House of Peter

Less well known is Jesus' visit to the house of Peter, recorded in Matthew 8:14–15 (cf. also Mark 1:29–31). "When Jesus came into Peter's house, He saw Peter's mother-in-law lying in bed with a fever. He touched her hand and the fever left her, and she got up and began to wait on Him." In other words, Jesus benefited from the hospitality of Peter and Peter's mother-in-law, probably in receiving a meal (that's why it says that she "began to wait on Him") and possibly in having a place to spend the night. Ralph Earle in *The Gospel according to Matthew* says some commentators think this is the house in mind in Matthew's Gospel when Jesus left a house prior to telling several parables and returned to the house later, where He explained one of them to the disciples (Matthew 13:1, 36).[3] This same house is probably also in view in Matthew 17:25, where Jesus asked Peter about the temple tax.

Jesus was apparently the guest of Peter on numerous occasions, with Peter as the giver of hospitality and Jesus the recipient. The day after Jesus healed Peter's mother-in-law, He "left the house and went off to a solitary place, where He prayed" (Mark 1:35). Obviously Jesus had been an overnight guest in the home of Peter. This same house may also be in view in Mark 7:17, for there Jesus appears to be in the vicinity of the Sea of Galilee (see Mark 6:45–56). Peter's house, which was in Capernaum, was probably the house where Jesus taught His disciples the concept of greatness in the kingdom (Mark 9:33–37). In fact, it may well be that the base of Jesus' ministry was Capernaum, in part, because He had a place there to stay. Though it is not clearly stated, many of the women who "cared for His needs" (Mark 15:41) probably provided Jesus many a meal and many a night's stay.

Unacceptable Houses

The Pharisees were aware of Jesus' practice of taking meals with unusual people, and, as a result, they complained about Jesus. At the banquet held by Matthew for Jesus, the Pharisees asked the disciples, "Why does your teacher eat with tax collectors and 'sinners'?" (Matthew 9:11). At the beginning of the great chapter on the lost sheep, the lost coin, and the lost son, we read, "But the Pharisees and the teachers of the law muttered, 'This man welcomes sinners and eats with them' " (Luke 15:2). Then Jesus told those three parables to express the joy in heaven over the sinner who repents, that is, the joy in heaven over the sinner who accepts the hospitality of the ultimate host, God. It should not surprise us that the shepherd who found the lost sheep went home, called his friends and neighbors together, and asked them to enjoy his hospitality in celebrating the finding of the lost sheep (Luke 15:6). Likewise the woman called her friends and neighbors together and asked them to enjoy her hospitality in celebrating the finding of the lost coin (Luke 15:9). Finally the father called his servants and family together and asked them to enjoy his hospitality in celebrating the finding of the lost son (Luke 15:22–24). Jesus sat at table with sinners because he was a friend of publicans and sinners. And is not the lost sheep (see also Matthew 18:10–14) the individual who has not been accepted into the fold of the Father? The lost sheep is one who has yet to know the loving hospitality of the God who created and redeemed all sheep.

The most well known of the unacceptable houses Jesus visited is that of Zacchaeus, to whom Jesus said, "Zacchaeus, come down immediately. I must stay at your house today" (Luke 19:5). The end of this story, to paraphrase Paul Harvey, was this statement from Jesus, "Today salvation has come to this house, because this man, too, is a son of Abraham. For the Son of Man came to seek and to save what was lost" (Luke 19:9–10). A few days later Jesus laid down His life for this man and for all others.

But notice something else about this story. By going to the house of Zacchaeus, Jesus took the time to move beyond the superficial. He chose to spend a significant amount of time with this despised tax collector, and He undoubtedly told Zacchaeus that God loved him as much as any other person in the world. William Hendriksen writes, "Is it not natural to believe also that to all those gathered there he spoke the words of life?"[4] Jesus probably shared a meal in the home of Zacchaeus. Zacchaeus, thrilled at the opportunity to have this well-known teacher in his home, must have broken bread with Jesus. But we can only speculate. We don't know the details; we only know the result.

In Matthew 11:19, Jesus acknowledged the criticism of His opponents. He said to His disciples and the crowd around Him, "The Son of Man came eating and drinking, and they say, 'Here is a glutton and a drunkard, a friend of tax collectors and "sinners" ' " (see also Luke 7:34). But, as Jesus had already told the Pharisees, "I have not come to call the righteous, but sinners" (Matthew 9:13).

A House at Emmaus

After the resurrection Jesus appeared to the Eleven as they were eating (Mark 16:14). After the trek to Emmaus, the two people who walked with Jesus would have missed out on the fellowship of Jesus' presence had they not extended hospitality to the one they thought to be a stranger; actually and ironically, they ended up enjoying *His* hospitality (Luke 24:13–35). Later, in the same chapter, Luke makes the point that by eating a piece of fish in the presence of the disciples, Jesus proved to the them that He was truly alive and not a ghost (Luke 24:36–43; see also John 21:9–13). Alan Loy McGinnis writes in *The Friendship Factor,* "It is no accident that so many important encounters occurred between Jesus and his friends when they were at table. There is something almost sacramental about breaking bread with one another."[5]

The House of a Certain Man

Jesus did host a sacramental meal—the Lord's Supper (Matthew 26:17–30; Mark 14:12–26; Luke 22:7–23). During that meal, arranged by Jesus to take place at the home of a friend (Matthew 26:18; Mark 14:14–15; Luke 22:10–12), the host wrapped a towel around His waist and washed the feet of His disciples (John 13:3–11). As has already been pointed out, foot-washing was an indication of the hospitality of the host, who was honoring the guests (1 Samuel 25:41; Luke 7:40–50; 1 Timothy 5:10). Through foot-washing, hosting a meal, and instituting a sacrament, Jesus again showed Himself as the ultimate host. .

The House of Nature

But that was not the first meal for which Jesus was the host. Yes, He enjoyed the hospitality of others, but He also extended hospitality. The feeding of the five thousand (Matthew 14:13–21; Mark 6:30–44; Luke 9:10–17; John 6:1–14) and the four thousand

(Matthew 15:29–39; Mark 8:1–10), both mentioned above, are times when Jesus entertained others with His miraculous powers. He simply did what a good host would do—He provided for His guests. Today He continues to feed His followers, for He is the bread of life who feeds millions spiritually as He once fed thousands both spiritually and physically. Then again, He feeds us physically today too, since all things come from His hands.

The House of Enemies

But Jesus shared meals with the religious leaders too. In Luke 7:36–50, Jesus shared a meal with a Pharisee. During that meal, Jesus rebuked the Pharisee while praising the sinful woman by stating three things the woman had done for Jesus which the Pharisee had not. The Pharisee had not given Jesus water for His feet, a kiss (the customary Middle Eastern sign of welcome), or oil for His head (to soothe the scalp in hot and dry weather). By these words, Jesus invites us not only to welcome people into our homes, but also to extend to them the signs of fellowship (a greeting at the door, help with coats, and the offer of a cool beverage on a hot day are common in American culture today). A few chapters later, in Luke 11:37–53, Jesus offered words of warning to the Pharisees while reclining at table to eat with them. This is one of the reasons that the Pharisees turned against Jesus—He actually took them to task while at one of their homes.

Keith Wright says, "Jesus knew a secret: Breaking bread breaks down barriers, strengthens relationships, and prepares people for wholeness. People love to eat! Food presentation doesn't need to be highly formal or extra fancy. Simply ask the Holy Spirit to bless your efforts, and bring on the food!"[6] A later session will make several suggestions that include meals, coffees, and desserts. The same practice that has been popular for church gatherings can also be effective in reaching out to those outside the Christian faith. After all, is not food something that Christians have in common with non-Christians?

And is not Jesus' sharing of meals a glimpse of the heavenly banquet that we will share in the kingdom of God? It is to the master's house that the servant invited "the poor, the crippled, the blind and the lame" (Luke 14:21) to enjoy the banquet which the invited guests (i.e., many of the Jewish people) had declined. Jesus also taught this elsewhere, for example, in the parable of the wedding banquet (Matthew 22:1–14) and the parable of the ten virgins who were invited to a wedding banquet (Matthew 25:1–13). Our Lord prepares a table before us, even in the presence of our enemies (Psalm 23:5), caring for our physical needs until the time He brings us directly into His presence.

In the Matter of Lodging

Jesus counted on the availability of homes for His own ministry and for that of the disciples. But even before He was born, while He was in the womb of Mary, He enjoyed the hospitality of Elizabeth (Luke 1:56). How different His ministry would have been without the hospitality of Mary and Martha and many of the other women who attended Him. Those with whom He stayed, such as Peter, were undoubtedly also those who provided Him with meals, so this section develops the concepts of the previous section. Actually, I don't think Jesus ever stayed anywhere without using that stay as an opportunity for teaching. When, for example, the Samaritans urged Jesus to stay with them, "He stayed two days. And because of His words many more became believers" (John 4:40–41). Consequently, the divisions within this session are somewhat artificial, for Jesus at times performed a miracle and taught at the same time or spent the night somewhere and used the occasion to teach or shared in a meal and used the occasion to teach the Word of God. There's a lesson in that for us as well.

Capernaum

The Gospels contain some indications that Jesus stayed with friends at various times. Most prominent, of course, is the house of Peter in Capernaum (Mark 1:29–37). Jesus spent a lot of time in Capernaum, His adopted home (Matthew 4:13; Mark 2:1). There He spent much time in the homes of other people as the recipient of their hospitality. Not only was Jesus willing to go to the home of the Roman army officer (Matthew 8:5–8), and not only did Peter open his home to Jesus in Capernaum, and not only did Jesus conduct much of His public ministry from Capernaum, but other significant events happened there, probably because this town was home for Jesus. There Jesus paid the temple tax (Matthew 17:24–27). There He taught in the synagogue (Mark 1:21; Luke

4:31). There He taught His disciples about greatness in the kingdom (Mark 9:33–37). There He went on numerous occasions to rest or to teach (John 2:12; 6:16–24, 59), so He must have spent many a night in the home of Peter.

Bethany

But also prominent is the city of Bethany, where Mary and Martha lived, as did Simon the leper, whose home Jesus also enjoyed at least once (Mark 14:3–10). At Bethany Jesus stayed after the triumphal entry into Jerusalem on Palm Sunday (Mark 11:1–11), just after He had gone to the temple and enjoyed the hospitality of His Father in that holy place. Mark 11:12 makes it clear that He spent the night there in Bethany. But John's Gospel also tells us that Jesus spent time in Bethany before Palm Sunday, probably a total of six days (John 12:1). At Bethany, a short time earlier, Jesus had raised Lazarus, also a resident of Bethany, from the dead (John 11).

At Bethany "a dinner was given in Jesus' honor" (John 12:2), where Mary anointed the feet of Jesus with a pint of expensive perfume (John 12:1–8; see also Matthew 26:6–13; Mark 14:3–9). From near Bethany, Jesus ascended to heaven (Luke 24:50).

The Towns and Villages of Israel

In Matthew 10:11–14, for example, Jesus taught the Twelve that, as they preached the message of the kingdom, they were to be dependent upon the worthy people of various towns and villages for hospitality. "Whatever town or village you enter, search for some worthy person there and stay at his house until you leave" (Matthew 10:11). The same is true for the sending out of the seventy-two (Luke 10:1–12). Donald Wayne Riddle says that the Twelve and the seventy-two "are instructed to take no money nor baggage with them. *For they are to assume the hospitality of the people to whom they proclaim their messages.*"[7]

When Lodging Is Denied

At the same time, however, Jesus warned that the hospitality of their own family members might well be denied His followers (Mark 10:29). But when that happens, Christians have the assurance that they now enjoy the hospitality of God "in this present age ... and in the age to come" (Mark 10:30), for they have become Jesus' followers for His sake and for the sake of the Gospel.

In Matthew 25:35, 45, we learn from Jesus' teaching that the sheep are separated from the goats on the principle of hospitality. The sheep provided strangers a place to stay and the goats did not.

We have seen that the practice of hospitality was important not only in significant portions of the Old and New Testaments. It was an important element in the life and teaching of Jesus, who adopted this practice of His culture and whose influence was felt in the various epistolary references to hospitality.

Jesus Christ, the great host, during His life on earth both enjoyed the hospitality of others and extended His hospitality to thousands. Further, He has indeed welcomed us into the earthly home He made for us. He has welcomed us also into the spiritual home, the church, which He has gathered together in His name. By His grace through faith in His death on the cross, He promises to welcome us one day into His Father's house and allow us to enjoy the ultimate in hospitality.

Discussion

1. Jesus shapes His people themselves into a house. How does Peter address this concept in 1 Peter 2:5?

2. Read Luke 5:30 and 15:2. What complaint do some of Jesus' contemporaries have against Him?

3. How does the Parable of the Unjust Steward touch on hospitality in Luke 16:4? Even the Parable of the Good Samaritan hints at the value of hospitality. How so? Read Luke 10:25–35.

4. Where did Jesus' first miracle take place? See John 2:1–11. Where did Jesus heal the mother-in-law of Peter? What else did he do there? See Matthew 8:14–17; Mark 1:29–34; Luke 4:38–41.

5. The familiar story of Mary listening to Jesus while Martha prepared the meal is set against the background of hospitality. What can you find in Luke 10:38–42 to indicate this? Put yourself in Martha's shoes. Would you have done differently? What does Luke mention in 10:40 that explains, without excusing, Martha's behavior?

6. How did the Pharisees feel about Jesus' practice of taking meals with unusual people? Read Matthew 9:11 and Luke 15:2. Next read Luke 19:9–10. How does hospitality play into this story in reverse? Why is it so significant that Jesus went to the house of Zacchaeus?

7. What did Jesus teach the disciples about hospitality in Matthew 10:11–14? And what did He teach the seventy-two in Luke 10:1–12?

8. Numerous ideas for offering hospitality have been discussed during previous weeks. Which of them have you actually carried out during the course of this Bible study? Can you share your story with the group?

Endnotes

1. William F. Arndt, *St. Luke* (St. Louis: Concordia Publishing House, 1956), 339.
2. Edith Schaeffer, "Hospitality: Optional or Commanded?" *Christianity Today* 29 (December 17, 1976): 29.
3. Ralph Earle, *The Gospel according to Matthew* (Kansas City: Beacon Hill Press), 129, 135.
4. William Hendriksen, *Exposition of the Gospel according to Luke* (Grand Rapids: Baker), 856.
5. Alan Loy McGinnis, *The Friendship Factor* (Minneapolis: Augsburg, 1979), 54.
6. Keith D. Wright, "Extending the Welcome Mat," *Evangelism* 10, no. 3 (May 1996): 103.
7. Donald Wayne Riddle, "Early Christian Hospitality: A Factor in the Gospel Transmission," *Journal of Biblical Literature* 57 (1938): 153.

Session 4 The Spiritual Gift of Hospitality

*W*ith *robber's hands my hospitable favours*
You should not ruffle thus. William Shakespeare, *King Lear*

Spiritual Gifts

Many have written on the subject of spiritual gifts, and this session will not attempt to summarize or repeat what they have written. Nor will this session address the topic of the so-called sign gifts, such as tongues, miracles, healing, and the interpretation of tongues. But we do need to look at a definition of spiritual gifts, the definition of the gift of hospitality, and the place of hospitality within the outreach ministry of the church.

Karen Mains wrote an entire book on the subject of hospitality: *Open Heart, Open Home* (David C. Cook Publishing Co.), although the purpose of the book was not to link hospitality to the outreach ministry of the church, as is the case with this book. In an article for *Moody Monthly,* she later wrote, "True hospitality is a gift of the Spirit."[1] Some argue that since hospitality appears in one of the frequently cited gift lists (1 Peter 4:7–11, a section that includes one of the five key passages discussed earlier in this book), Scripture includes hospitality among the gifts of the Spirit. (One could convincingly argue on the basis of context, however, that this gift list actually begins in 1 Peter 4:10 and ends in 4:11. That would exclude the mention of hospitality in 4:9 from the gift list. Others would question whether this section of Scripture is actually a gift list.)

Some may question the inclusion of hospitality in a spiritual-gifts list. However, it finally matters very little, in the practical sense, whether or not hospitality is considered a spiritual gift. Hospitality is certainly an attitude that shows itself in practical ways in the home especially, and many people are hospitable whether they are gifted for hospitality or not. Furthermore, a non-Christian can be

56

hospitable. If hospitality looks similar when practiced by a Christian or a non-Christian, then we must either recognize that hospitality is not a spiritual gift or we must see the spiritual gift of hospitality as different from the hospitality of the non-Christian in the motivation, the very precise ways in which the gift is exercised (for example, with traveling missionaries, guest preachers, and the like), when the gift is bestowed, and in the blessing of God upon hospitality. Even if 1 Peter 4:9 is not part of a list of spiritual gifts, hospitality could still be a God-given gift, though not a spiritual gift, for use both in the family of God and by the family of God for the benefit of those outside that family.

So what are spiritual gifts? Spiritual gifts are "particular manifestations of the Holy Spirit (1 Cor[inthians] 12:7) that call the members of the church to action in a manner that confesses Christ and builds up the body of Christ. These gifts or manifestations of the Spirit may take the form of activities, abilities, offices, roles, and even people."[2] The fact that a spiritual gift confesses Christ suggests its relationship to evangelism. By confessing Christ, even to the non-Christian, a spiritual gift builds up the body of Christ because that member of the body exercises a gift as God intended. The gift of hospitality would fit within the words *activities, abilities,* and *roles* in the definition above, especially the word *abilities,* as we will see shortly.

What must concern every Christian who seeks to help Christians exercise their spiritual gifts is that we not replace the God-given means by which the Holy Spirit normally works, the means of grace—God's Word and Sacraments. When Christians perceive spiritual gifts as the source of spiritual power rather than God Himself, then we have shifted our focus away from God, away from divine power, away from the means through which the Holy Spirit works, to human activities. We have focused on human works rather than the work of God.

The Gift of Hospitality

So how do those who regard hospitality as a spiritual gift define this gift? C. Peter Wagner, paraphrasing Leslie Flynn, defines it this way: "The gift of hospitality is that special ability that God gives to certain members of the body of Christ to provide open house and warm welcome for those in need of food and lodging."[3] Bruce Bugbee defines hospitality as "the divine enablement to care for people by providing fellowship, food, and shelter."[4]

Wagner describes the kind of people who don't have the gift and those who do. He claims that those who don't have the gift "want everything to be in place, rugs clean, furniture dusted, toys and newspapers picked up, fresh-cut flowers on the tables, candlelight, and the food something special, prepared and served just right."[5] People who have the gift, he says, can welcome someone into unsightly rooms without apology. One might wonder whether it is impossible for the person who wants everything in place to be hospitable. At the same time, does this mean that those whose homes are "unsightly" are in reality more likely to be hospitable? Certainly "those with the gift always have the comfort of the visitor as their highest priority."[6] Francis and Edith Schaeffer of L'Abri, Switzerland, had the gift, many would say. But even those who seemingly aren't good at being hospitable can entertain people in the home.

In the *Personal Renewal Study* of the Department of Stewardship and Financial Support of The Lutheran Church—Missouri Synod, people with the gift of hospitality are described in this way:

> **Persons with the gift of hospitality enjoy having strangers in their home... . Christians who have the gift of hospitality warmly welcome into their home, for the glory of God and the growth of the Church, those who are in need of food and a place to stay. They are happier with guests in their homes than they are without. They are neither embarrassed by a cluttered house nor strained by an indefinite stay, but instead develop with their guests a special bond of Christian fellowship that builds unity within the body of Christ.[7]**

The gift of hospitality, then, is the ability of Christians to open their homes to other people, particularly strangers (remember the literal definition of the New Testament word), whether for the purpose of building up the body of Christ or for the purpose of reaching out with the Gospel or both. Later in this book, however, I will argue that there are many other ways to show love for the stranger. The home is the first place, I believe, intended by the New Testament teaching, but we can love the stranger at our churches, and we can love the stranger in the stranger's home, neighborhood, or community.

Evangelism and Hospitality

One of the most obvious benefits of hospitality is that it enables those who will never make an evangelism call, are timid about sharing their faith, are introverted, and think of themselves as lacking the gift of evangelism (Ephesians 4:11) to invite people into their homes and demonstrate the love of Christ by their warmth, friendliness, and openness. Further, it enables them to practice hospitality when guests worship at their church, when new neighbors move in, when they have the opportunity to bring a hot meal to a family in need, and in a host of other ways. These people can truly love others until those others ask them why.

The back cover of *Who Cares about Love?* states, "Startling new research illustrates that loving churches are growing churches." The concept is not all that new any more, but it is new to many people. In the book *Who Cares about Love?* Win Arn, Carroll Nyquist, and Charles Arn show the relationship between love, closely akin to hospitality, as the word *hospitality* itself indicates, and the outreach ministry of the church.[8] The book contains the tabulated results from a Love/Care Quotient (LCQ), seventeen questions that were sent to churches of various denominations, sizes, geographical areas, styles of ministry, and membership patterns. A total of 8,658 people from 168 churches of thirty-nine denominations participated by answering the questions about themselves.

One question they answered was this: "On a scale of 1–10, how 'loving' have you been to the following persons: spouse, parents, other family, pastor, other church members, close friends, neighbors, school/work associates?"[9] As one might expect, spouses came in the highest at 8.7. Participants in the questionnaire scored parents at 8.2, family at 8.1, close friends at 7.5, their pastor at 6.9, church members at 6.5, school and work associates at 5.9, and neighbors at 5.5.[10] Similar results were tabulated in response to the question "On a scale of 1–10, how 'loved' do you feel by the following persons: spouse, parents, other family, pastor, other church members, close friends, neighbors, school/work associates?"[11]

But what does this have to do with hospitality? Remember that the New Testament word for hospitality, *philoxenia,* literally means "love for the stranger." Remember also that the word *phileo,* which is the first half of *philoxenia,* in its original sense is defined by the *Theological Dictionary of the New Testament* (9:115; Eerdmans) as "to regard and treat somebody as one of one's own people." The Christian practice of hospitality takes place when a Christian treats a stranger as though that stranger were one of his or her own people. The practice of hospitality is also more likely carried out by those who are filled with the love of God in Christ Jesus. "We love because He first loved us" (1 John 4:19). The practice of hospitality, the love of the stranger, more likely and more frequently happens when people are moved, shaped, and forgiven by the love of God in Christ Jesus.

Discussion

1. The gift lists appear in Romans 12:4–8; 1 Peter 4:7–11; 1 Corinthians 12:7–11, 27–31; and Ephesians 4:7–13. In how many of those lists does hospitality appear?

2. Look at 1 Peter 4:7–11. Could hospitality be considered to be one of the gifts mentioned in this list? Why or why not?

3. Evaluate the argument against considering hospitality a spiritual gift.

4. What difference might it make if we considered hospitality not to be a spiritual gift?

5. Do you agree that people who can welcome someone into a messy room are more hospitable than others? Why?

6. How might you demonstrate hospitality in unique ways to others?

Endnotes

1. Karen Mains, "Hospitality Means More Than a Party," *Moody Monthly* (December 1976): 38.
2. *Spiritual Gifts,* A Report of the Commission on Theology and Church Relations of The Lutheran Church—Missouri Synod, September 1994 (St. Louis: The Lutheran Church—Missouri Synod, 1995), 43.
3. C. Peter Wagner, *Your Spiritual Gifts Can Help Your Church Grow* (Glendale, Calif.: Regal Books, 1979), 70.
4. Bruce Bugbee, *What You Do Best in the Body of Christ* (Grand Rapids: Zondervan, 1995), 61.
5. Wagner, *Your Spiritual Gifts Can Help Your Church Grow,* 71.
6. Wagner, *Your Spiritual Gifts Can Help Your Church Grow,* 71.
7. *Personal Renewal Study* (St. Louis: Department of Stewardship and Financial Support, The Lutheran Church—Missouri Synod, 1984), 51.
8. Win Arn, Carroll Nyquist, and Charles Arn, *Who Cares about Love?* (Monrovia, Calif.: Church Growth Press, 1986), 61, 62, 64, 118, 129, 138–45.
9. Arn, Nyquist, and Arn, *Who Cares about Love?* 61.
10. Arn, Nyquist, and Arn, *Who Cares about Love?* 62.
11. Arn, Nyquist, and Arn, *Who Cares about Love?* 16.

Session 5 The Practical Application

*B*ut give me ... the half wild, yet frank and hospitable *manners.* Washington Irving, *The Alhambra*

So now what? Just exactly how do we love others until they ask us why? Perhaps you are naturally hospitable. And perhaps you aren't, but you're willing to be hospitable for the sake of Christ. Just how, practically, can this happen?

Before we try to practice hospitality, we must first love people. Love God and then love people. Those are the two tables of the Law. We want to live a life of love because God has loved us first through His Son.

Three Levels of Hospitality

Hospitality can be demonstrated at three different levels. After all, hospitality literally means "love for the stranger," and one can express that love to a stranger in a variety of ways and a variety of settings. The first is the *family level* of hospitality, which literally provides an open house and warm welcome to those who need food and a place to stay. But it also provides an open house and warm welcome to those in need of friendship. The second is the *congregational level* of hospitality, which provides an open house and warm welcome to the sanctuary or other part of the church facility through some form of ministry. This level also operates when members, as a part of an organized congregational effort, invite neighbors into their homes for a home Bible study or other organized ministry. Third, the *community level* of hospitality provides a warm welcome to the community. This third level is provided by the community itself when an organization such as Welcome Wagon brings gifts to the new family. It is provided by the church when, as a member of the community, it sends newcomers a letter of welcome to the community, it sends visitors to meet newcomers, or it offers a service to the community or meets a community need, such as Mothers' Day Out or the Car Care Clinic that one Wyoming church offered. Hospitality, whether practiced in your home, in your church home, or in your community, affects the ability of the church to reach out with the Gospel.

The Practice of Hospitality in Your Personal Life—The Family Level

On Sunday, May 13, 1990, I had the privilege of baptizing into the Christian faith a Japanese student by the name of Yuka Miyazawa. My family and I first got acquainted with her when we invited her to spend Thanksgiving vacation of 1989 with us. She got very well acquainted with my daughter Brenda, and the two became good friends. Then, later that semester, she came to me and asked about the Christian faith. I arranged for her to be instructed in the Christian faith at my home congregation during the spring semester. When she had nearly completed her instruction, she asked that I perform the Baptism. I was honored!

During the time we got to know her, we also learned about her friendship with another Japanese student, a young Christian from Sapporo by the name of Izumi Osawa. Robert Kolb calls this tag-team evangelism. Izumi was one member of the team, and my family and I were other members. Still other Christians, some at Concordia University Wisconsin and perhaps others in other places about whom I do not know even to this day, were part of the same tag-team. As Paul wrote, "I planted the seed, Apollos watered it, but God made it grow" (1 Corinthians 3:6). But it was the friendships established with Yuka, some of them in a Christian home, that provided the setting within which the Gospel could be shared, and Yuka is a practicing Christian to this day, active in her local church in Tokyo, Japan.

At one point in his life, C. T. Studd was considered by many to be England's greatest cricket player. Later he became a missionary to China and then to the Belgian Congo. He was also a leader of the Student Volunteer Movement of the late nineteenth and early twentieth centuries, a movement that saw tens of thousands of young people volunteer for missionary service. C. T. Studd once said, "Some wish to live within the sound of church bells. I want to build my rescue mission within a yard of hell." You and I may not become missionaries, but we need to hear that message and apply it in our own neighborhoods. We need to be willing to meet those people whose lifestyles we disagree with. We need to be willing to put up with some of their bad habits and ungodly behavior long enough to get acquainted and perhaps reach them. It may be a stretch for us at first, but we can learn, for the sake of the salvation of people whom God loves and for whom Christ died, to open our hearts, our homes, our churches, our lives to others. We can love them until they ask us why.

Keith Wright argues that the hospitable person has four important characteristics: (1) preparation; (2) cheerfulness; (3) zeal; and (4) generosity.[1] I would argue for a fifth characteristic: humility.

Preparation is necessary, since the opportunity to be hospitable can come at unexpected times. The person who suddenly needs a place to stay for just one night is probably more unprepared than the host, but the hospitable host can meet that need.

> Several years ago, [writes Keith Wright,] stranded 500 miles from home, I reluctantly drove to a nearby church parking lot to camp out in my car. As I unrolled a sleeping bag in the back seat, the church's youth pastor walked across the parking lot. Not wanting me to spend the night in a car, he invited me, a complete stranger, to sleep at his house. He offered me a bed and served a warm breakfast in the morning. He was ready to show hospitality at a moment's notice.[2]

Cheerfulness indicates that God is at work in the Christian's life. Laughter helps people to feel at ease, especially when they are afraid that they are putting you out. They are also more willing to listen to a life-changing message when they do not feel threatened.

Zeal means that hospitality is not something that merely happens. When we love God and our fellow human beings, we look for opportunities to be hospitable. As Paul wrote, "Practice hospitality" (Romans 12:13), words which mean "pursue hospitality" intentionally.

The value of **generosity** is obvious. Christians who extend hospitality must not expect to be paid back. If they do, they probably approach the exercise of hospitality as a duty rather than a privilege. They have failed to allow the divine love of *agape* to transform the friendship love of *philia*. God is so generous to us; our payback in the exercise of hospitality carries far greater rewards than any normal reimbursement, and it could include the salvation of a single soul.

Humility is important, because its opposite, pride, cannot make the stranger feel welcome in our home. Erwin Lutzer has written, "Hospitality is a test for godliness because those who are selfish do not like strangers (especially needy ones) to intrude upon their private lives. They prefer their own friends who share their life-style. Only the humble have the necessary resources to give of themselves to those who could never give of themselves in return."[3]

Here is an example of a hospitable couple: Recently a church hosted an informal gathering at a couple's home where a local Christian counselor spoke on the subject of establishing harmony in the home. The host couple's spacious living room was filled with a mixture of people from the neighborhood, new attendees of the church, friends of members, as well as members themselves. The reason for the positive response was the topic, which addressed a question that people were asking. The answer to the question was biblical and practical, including the Good News of forgiveness through Jesus Christ. Those who planned the gathering scratched where people itched.[4]

A Potpourri of Ideas

Most people who enjoy practicing hospitality don't have to think about how they are going to be hospitable. However, for some people hospitality comes more slowly. For them the following list may help in their practice of hospitality. For others, this "potpourri of ideas" may help them to learn to be hospitable to others for the first time. One of the implications of a list like this is that people practice hospitality in different ways. You need not fit into someone else's mold.

1. Love, the first half of hospitality. Love them until they ask you why. You've read those words many times in these pages. Let them stick deep within your heart with a Spirit-inspired glue.

2. Lunch. Invite an unbeliever to lunch. Yes, that's right. It doesn't sound very evangelistic, but then, the purpose of this book is to bring evangelism within the reach of every concerned Christian. Expect this book to break some of the stereotypes.

This lunch doesn't have to happen in your home, although that's an excellent place. You could invite one of your colleagues at work out to an area restaurant for lunch, just as a gesture of friendship. Another exciting option is to make an agreement with your spouse to invite a non-Christian family or couple over for supper once a month for the next twelve months. You need not have an agenda; just have them over for a meal. The conversation does not need to cover the basics of the Christian faith. You may talk about whatever you please. Your goal is to make friends with one or two people over a meal. Consider inviting some of these people back; you don't have to invite twelve different couples or families during the year. Add prayer to the mix, and wait for God to open a door for your conversation. Love them until they ask you why. Better yet, don't do this on your own. In order to provide you with some accountability, enter an agreement with another couple for each of the two couples to do this. Pray for one another, check with each other monthly, and find out how it's going with the other couple. You'll more likely follow through on your commitment if you know that you're going to talk about it with a friend.

Your home will witness for you, too, if you have Christian art and symbolism on the walls or Christian literature on the coffee table. While we ought not to rely on those unspoken messages, we can still set the stage for our witness or arouse curiosity about our priorities and beliefs. The best kind of stage-setter is the provocative piece of artwork or needlepoint that invites a question or arouses curiosity. When they ask, simply tell them.

Jesus ate numerous meals with unbelievers. Jesus actually had the practice of taking meals with unusual people, as we noted earlier. Some people talk about "cold turkey" evangelism, the kind that makes "cold calls" on people the callers have never met. Here I am advocating "hot turkey" evangelism, that is, inviting people into your home for a meal, perhaps even a meal of cooked turkey, with the goal of getting better acquainted with them. Perhaps God will open a door for a conversation about the faith in the process.

3. Home gatherings. Have non-Christian people into your home on a regular basis for any reason whatever. Too many Christians have few or no non-Christian friends. Build relationships with non-Christians by having them into your home for meals, for a Super Bowl party, for your daughter's piano concert, or for a cold glass of lemonade on a hot summer day.

4. **Funny cards**. Send funny cards on occasions other than the ususal ones, such as Groundhog Day. In 1997, I received Groundhog Day cards from six different people, all of them members of Immanuel Lutheran Church, Winnipeg, Manitoba, the church at

which I first presented these concepts about hospitality. It is to the people of that church that this book is dedicated. John and Carol Cullen, my hosts during the conference, were among those who sent cards. They are the ones whose hospitality I enjoyed at the family level, along with their son Tim. Their granddaughter Marci and daughter Tessa were among those whose hospitality I enjoyed at the congregational level. Those kinds of cards are not normally sent, but Groundhog Day and other unusual occasions can be used to make the contact. A friend and former student of mine, Wayne Huebner, sends me a Hanukkah card every year. He is not Jewish, nor am I. But I am Wayne's former Hebrew teacher.

5. Holiday get-togethers. Hold a Christmas party, a Thanksgiving gathering (many people have simply too many Christmas gatherings to attend), a Fourth of July event, or some other holiday meeting.

6. Block party. Organize a block party for your neighborhood. It's a lot of work, but you have the opportunity to grow friendships that you might not otherwise have. You don't have to invite everyone if you don't want to put in the time. Just invite a few families for a combined backyard barbecue.

7. Welcome party. Hold a welcome party for a new resident. So many people are wrapped up in their own worlds that they don't even welcome new people who move in next door. Why not break the ice, meet those new people, and provide an occasion for neighbors to meet them, too, in the comfy confines of your house, complete with refreshments? It might be the beginning of a friendship with these new residents that could result in a witness.

8. Slide show. Hold a travelogue slide show and invite your neighbors, provided, of course, that your slides captivate rather than bore. Or invite your neighbors to bring their slides to your house and *show* you *theirs*. Now there's an idea!

9. Dinner for eight. People can conduct this ministry on their own or as a part of an organized congregational ministry. At First Christian Church, Medford, Oregon, three of the active families and three prospective families were invited to the pastor's home. During the evening they got acquainted. The heart of the evening included the testimony of the members about what excited them about the church. Sixteen of eighteen adults came into the church as a result of these meetings.[5]

A similar approach is that of Sandy Springs Christian Church, Atlanta, Georgia. Two couples who recently joined the church, two couples who have visited the church, a couple that has been in the church for a longer period of time, and the pastor and spouse meet in the home of one of the member couples. After dessert and coffee, conversation, and mixing, the pastor leads a directed conversation about a meaningful faith. Nothing is mentioned in these meetings about joining the church, but the prospective members who attend these gatherings have joined the church at a rate of approximately ninety percent.[6]

But you don't have to have that agenda. Getting some people together for a meal, some of them Christians and some not, will build the kinds of bridges—in homes and over a meal—that may one day bear fruit for eternity.

10. Fondue party. Keith Wright writes, appropriately, "Who can resist chocolate? Invite a group over with the explicit invitation to 'Fondue and a Discussion of the Christian Faith.' Enjoy socializing and dessert. Then have a spiritually mature person make a ten-minute presentation on the relevance of a relationship with Christ. Open a discussion time for guests to ask questions."[7] Variations could include barbecues, coffee-tasting parties, or burrito bars.

11. Literary society. Similar to a book club, participants read and discuss books or other selected readings, sometimes works by Christian authors and sometimes not. An atmosphere of intellectual honesty will enable both Christians and non-Christians to stretch their thinking.[8]

12. For college students only: befriend the two loneliest groups of students on every college campus, the freshmen during their first few weeks and international students. Invite such students into your room, take them with you to town, show them around, sightsee, and so on. You are the host of the freshman if you are a sophomore, junior, or senior. You are the host of the international student if you are a citizen of this country. Or, if you often go home on the weekend, do something strange. Stay in the residence hall one weekend and build bridges to the non-Christians in your residence hall wing.

13. Bruce Lieske writes about a number of activities, all of which could be practiced on an individual level or at the congregation level.

"Free babysitting for a friend
Inviting a visiting pastor or missionary into your home
    for a meal
Taking a hot meal to somebody who is ill

Finding a job for somebody
Providing transportation to the doctor for a sick person
Providing clothing for a family whose home has burned
Inviting a Sunday morning visitor to your home for a meal
Resettling a Vietnamese family."[9]

As Lieske's last suggestion and my story about Yuka Miyazawa indicate, international students who are attending college in the United States are among the people most willing to listen to our witness and hear about our faith. By opening our homes and by allowing them to see how we live and what we believe, these students catch a glimpse of the glory of God.

For three weeks in August 1997, our family hosted a young French student by the name of Arnaud as part of an international experience for French teenagers. We were his family for that length of time, providing housing, food, companionship, and the opportunity for him to develop his already considerable ability to speak the English language. It didn't take long for him to notice that the Christian faith was an important part of our family life. During a gathering we hosted in our home for friends who had spent a semester in London with us, he approached my wife, Cheryl, and wanted to talk about Christianity. He especially got close to our oldest, Peter, who is approximately the same age. We have since purchased a modern language French version of the Bible and sent it to him. We keep in contact through e-mail, now that he has returned to France, and we include him regularly in our prayers.

But remember one other point made in the introductory session. Ted Engstrom and his wife were both the recipients of hospitality and the givers of hospitality in their friendship with Khang and Thu Lee. Christians are not always the givers. They do not carry on their service for the Lord from an attitude of superiority, but as fellow sinners with the same need for forgiveness as anyone else. Sometimes the God-given humility of a Christian who is willing to benefit from the hospitality of the non-Christian provides the open door for sharing the Gospel of Jesus Christ.

The Practice of Hospitality in the Local Church—The Congregational Level

What would a congregation that practices hospitality look like? How would its members respond to the needs in the community for fellowship, friendship, caring, and other meaningful relationships? In short, how would they function as the body of Christ? How would they love people in their community until those people asked them why? While session 6 will give you a look at several specific churches and their ministry of hospitality, this next section will provide some general ideas of the practice of hospitality in the local church.

In his book *The Problem of Wineskins,* Howard Snyder describes the condition of many Christian churches that do not experience the kind of fellowship "of and in" the Holy Spirit as in New Testament times. The church is more of an institution than a community of believers. He writes:

> One seldom finds within the institutionalized church today that winsome intimacy among people where masks are dropped, honesty prevails, and there is that sense of communication and community beyond the human—where there is literally the fellowship of and in the Holy Spirit.[10]

Bruce Lieske writes similarly, "What does your congregation consider 'Christian fellowship' to be? Often congregations equate it with potluck suppers, Sunday school socials, church picnics, and other such gatherings where the conversation is about jobs, families, sports, and hobbies."[11] Lieske goes on to suggest that a congregation that practices a biblical fellowship among its members will spontaneously practice hospitality.

So there is room for improvement in the fellowship practices of the Christian churches of America, improvement that will include the practice of hospitality and meaningful relating to one another through the medium of the Word of God. Such a practice will also have an outward focus, including in our activities the worship guest, whose presence many Christians are not prepared for and, in reality, do not welcome or do not welcome well.

The Myth of Greeters

Unfortunately, many congregations think they are doing their duty of Christian hospitality by assigning greeters to welcome people to church when they arrive on a Sunday morning. Hardly. Greeters usually only enable a congregation to fall into what Eugene Heideman, in his article "Alone at the After-Worship Coffeepot," calls "the pitfall of superficial inclusion."[12] Greeters too easily encourage congregations to think that they are being hospitable to those who are guests at worship, while, in reality, they have little time for the outsider.

This is the unspoken myth of greeters that must be exploded: *Greeters provide guests who worship with us all the friendliness that they want or need.*

Congregations that want to make their place of worship or their home Bible study or some other hospitality ministry (listed below) truly welcoming must avoid Heideman's three pitfalls:

1. The pitfall of unfocused purpose
2. The pitfall of unintentional exclusion
3. The pitfall of superficial inclusion

The *unfocused purpose* is the invitation for guests to enjoy the fellowship of the congregation when the actual purpose is to provide opportunities for the members to meet each other. *Unintentional exclusion* sometimes results when members are shy with strangers, but comfortable with old friends. Church members are friendly, to be sure, but they are often only friendly to their friends. Strangers are not welcome. No love for the stranger at those churches. The *superficial inclusion* is the exchange of names, the shaking of hands, and the brief conversation. This inclusion is polite, but most people who visit a new church are looking for far more than simple politeness.

Joe Harding tells the story of a church in the state of Washington that broke through the pitfall of superficial inclusion and the myth of greeters simultaneously. This church plotted on a chart the places where certain members sat each Sunday. After the benediction one Sunday, these members remained behind for a brief meeting. They were asked to scan their pew each Sunday, as well as the pew in front of them and the pew behind them. Immediately after the benediction each Sunday, their job was to meet the visitors in that part of the church and introduce them to another member. "Each Sunday one of the section greeters waits by the door to invite the first-time visitor to be his or her guest for Sunday dinner. Once visitors receive an invitation to Sunday dinner, they return and join the church."[13]

If you have greeters, continue to have them. But don't rely on them exclusively. Explain to the congregation that greeters are simply a safety net, designed to make sure that no one slips through the cracks, enters, worships, and leaves without ever speaking to a member. People should introduce themselves to those who sit near them. The coffeepot should be a place where members look first to meet someone new and second to renew old acquaintances.

A Potpourri of Ideas

Here are some additional suggestions about the practice of hospitality in a church's ministry. Some of them are obviously amenable to the practice of hospitality, while others would need to include hospitality intentionally. Many of these are what Larry Gilbert calls AMEs, that is, Acquaintance Making Events. At these events, usually some sort of a social gathering or small group, the non-Christian has the opportunity to meet some Christians. Others are what Gilbert calls RSAs, that is, Relationship Strengthening Activities. The AME is the introduction of the non-Christian to some Christian people in a social context, while the RSA is the cultivating of the relationship to the point of a friendship.[14] The RSA is more one-on-one, and the more relationships that are cultivated the better.

1. Small group ministry, including home Bible studies. Arnell Arn and Jerry Jamison advocate the use of small groups as a follow-up to something like a parenting seminar. This will turn a need-meeting ministry, such as a parenting seminar, into an opportunity to show hospitality to the non-Christian in a home setting.[15]

2. Encouragement to believe that ministry can be done at a barbecue, church picnic, cookout, party, or potluck.

3. Fellowship with an eye on evangelism. One example of this is the evangelism coffees that have taken place at First Christian Church, Noblesville, Indiana. Informal coffees for members and prospective members took place in member homes on Sunday evenings from 6:00 to 8:00 p.m. every two months. Each evangelism committee member brought a dessert, and the host provided coffee, tea, and other drinks. Dessert was served at the beginning, and a time of unstructured fellowship ensued. Members and prospects then told the group something about themselves. The minister or a committee member spent some time talking about the history and beliefs of the Christian church. Time was allowed for questions and personal sharing of the faith. At the close of the gathering, each prospective person or couple received a card on which they were invited to set a date for uniting with the church.[16]

4. Coffee and cookies served between and after services and before or after Bible classes, with a concern for using the fellowship time to meet people we don't already know.

5. Greeters (in spite of what I wrote earlier). Greeters perform a useful function, but they dare not lull us into thinking that they are surrogate greeters for the rest of the congregation.

6. Church softball team, bowling team, basketball team, dartball team, and so forth. When non-Christians are invited to play on an athletic team, the church is saying, "Be a part of our family, at least in this way. Perhaps you'll want to be a part of our family in other ways in the future."

7. Invitations to all sorts of church events.

8. Prayer meetings. This may sound strange to some, but others will find it quite natural to invite non-Christians friends, many of whom pray, to attend such a meeting where their specific needs will be prayed for.

9. Worship services that have an eye on the guest. Most churches worship as though they were expecting no one except members to show up. Friendly ushers, helpful signs, worship services printed out in full in the bulletin, a pastor who makes guests feel at home, members who look for new faces to meet, an explanation of the theme of the day, invitations to activities of the coming week, and many other practices display a hospitable approach in a worship setting.

10. Friendship Sunday, when coupled with a hospitable atmosphere. Already in 1982 Central Christian Church, Waco, Texas, held Bring-a-Friend Sundays, which followed worship with a lunch that was free to visitors. During the following week, those who were guests at worship received a packet of information about the congregation and a welcome letter. Follow-up on those who returned for a second time included an invitation to the parsonage for lunch on Sunday or dessert on a weeknight. The invitations to the pastor's home were considered to be of the utmost importance.[17] Celebration of Friendship, Friend Day, The Second Day, and F.R.A.N.tastic Days are all program materials for this approach called Friendship Sunday or Open House Sunday.

11. Thank-you letter. Most people send thank you notes for gifts they received. Churches who have guests on Sunday receive a gift—the gift of the presence of those persons. A thank you note is an appropriate and hospitable response to their worship attendance.

12. Invite a worship guest for lunch. Ken Zorn tells the story of a pastor by the name of John Frase of Ontario, Canada. Pastor Frase told of a new couple who worshipped at his church and whom he invited to lunch at his home after church. The man started laughing, and Pastor Frase said, "What's wrong? What are you laughing at? What's so funny?" The man said, "This is some church! I walked down the aisle, and I had six invitations for lunch. You're the seventh." Guess which church they joined.[18]

13. The previous section included the idea that couples make an agreement to invite a non-Christian family or couple over for supper once a month for the next twelve months. A church could implement that idea at the congregational level by keeping records of those commitments, the suppers, the contacts between couples who have covenanted together, and so on.

The Practice of Hospitality in the Local Church—The Community Level

Lyle Schaller says that "community has moved out of the neighborhood and into the marketplace."[19] If that is true, then we must look to provide community (a sense of togetherness) not only in our homes or at our church, but we must also provide community by practicing hospitality out in the marketplace, especially in the urban centers of our country. We must be hospitable as a community (a population center, that is, a city, town, or village) to people who live in the same town or village.

Some communities are hospitable, while others are not. Some communities welcome new people to town, through a Welcome Wagon or some such program, or simply through the friendliness of the people. That's hospitality. When churches practice hospitality at the community level, they welcome new residents, display friendliness as members of the community, and meet the needs of their community in ways and at places that are usually apart from the church's regular programming. The church offers hospitality at the community level when, as a member of the community, it sends a letter of welcome to newcomers, sends visitors to meet newcomers, or offers a service to the community that meets a community need, such as Mothers' Day Out. This is feeding people when they are hungry, visiting them when they are in prison, inviting strangers into your home, and looking after the sick (Matthew 25:35–40).

When members of the church welcome new residents to the community who have just moved into their neighborhood, they are practicing hospitality at the community level. A hospitable church in Casper, Wyoming, for example, holds an annual Car Care Clinic, where members change oil and oil filters, check fluid levels and air pressure on tires, and so on, free of charge for single mothers. This hospitality is carried out by the local church at the community level because the church, as a member of the community, is meeting a need in the community rather than offering a church program. The church does so with unconditional love, insisting that it will meet this need, whether or not people in the community become Christians or join the church as a result.

Vineyard Community Church, Cincinnati, Ohio, offers dozens of these types of ministries, some of which are mentioned below. These ministries, done out of love with no expectation of anything in return, are truly "love for the stranger." As a result, Vineyard, under the leadership of Pastor Steve Sjogren, is one of the twenty-five fastest growing churches in the United States. The members of this church have truly learned to love others until they ask why.

So how can a church practice hospitality toward its community? Here are several additional ways.

A Potpourri of Ideas

1. A letter of welcome to the community. Many churches send these welcome letters to new residents, offering additional information about the church, but also providing helpful information about the community that newcomers might otherwise have difficulty discovering. How do you register to vote? Where are the public libraries located? What doctors and dentists are taking new patients? Where is the nearest post office? Where can I buy _____ (fill in the blank)? Where do I go to get new license plates and a driver's license?

2. Visiting newcomers to the community. Many churches also send people to the homes of new residents with a word of welcome as a way of following up on their letter. An invitation to worship services, a printed handout about the church's ministry, or a friendly time of sharing about the new community can open doors.

3. Welcome Wagon. You might choose to get involved in the local Welcome Wagon program, if there is one, or start one of your

own, if there isn't. This welcome especially shows hospitality to the community as a whole.

4. Days out for moms with preschoolers. This program has been around for a long time, and many churches have offered this to the community. It shows hospitality to the community by meeting the need of moms for free time and by providing a place for the preschooler that is safe and secure.

5. Support groups for the bereaved. Those who have lost a spouse often need someone to talk to, someone who understands the situation, and someone who will uphold confidentiality.

6. Project days to help the elderly. Churches that provide free labor to the elderly who are unable to make minor household repairs or even carry out major projects will love them until the elderly ask them why.

7. Classes for new parents. The one task in life for which people are least prepared is parenthood. Seldom do parents realize this, however, until the first child has arrived. These classes, taught by experienced parents, can meet an important need in the community.

8. Support groups for divorce recovery. Everyone has heard the statistics (usually incorrectly reported) about the percentage of marriages that end in divorce. The church can show its concern for the community by providing a place not just for divorcees to vent their feelings, but to find meaningful help, informed by Scripture.

9. Visitation in nursing homes. Churches that conduct services in nursing homes or visit with the aged can send another signal to the community: "We care about those whose medical condition or health and age make it difficult or impossible for family members to care for them."

10. Classes on self-concept. The most important aspect of self-concept is to know that Jesus Christ has redeemed me. Where else will people discover this idea than in a Christian church?

11. Retreats for marriage enrichment. Before marriages begin to crumble, they can grow strong, especially in the first few years of marriage, where the risk of failure is greater.

12. Services or Bible classes in jails. Just as nursing home visitation sends a message, so also do visitation, worship services, and Bible classes in jails. Prison Fellowship is the most visible organization that does this kind of work, and it has seen many prisoners come to faith in Christ, but there are many other organizations with similar goals.

13. Building projects for the underprivileged. Habitat for Humanity is one organization that seeks to meet needs in the community, although not in the name of Jesus Christ. Churches that sign on to Habitat for Humanity or carry out other similar projects will get a reputation in the community as churches that really care about people.

14. Tutoring programs for high school students. Many large cities have major problems in their schools. Many other schools have succumbed to the modern ideologies that have sapped the strength of education in America. Teaching students to read well can make a major contribution to the education of high school students or elementary school students or early childhood students, since reading is usually the major problem of students who are failing. Equip a few of your members with the phonetic method of teaching reading, and you will help the people of your community. Get them hooked on phonics.

15. Twelve step groups for alcoholics. Alcoholics Anonymous and other related groups need a place to meet. The church should be one of the places open to their work, especially when groups like AA are based on spiritual principles.

16. Seminars for stress management. Stress has been called the disease of modernity. Perhaps you can offer solutions to this disease and find health professionals to present seminars on managing stress.

17. Seminars on changing jobs. As our complex economy changes, many people must change jobs to adjust. Churches that invite professionals to conduct these seminars, whether they are Christians or not, can meet another important need in society. Such seminars could include a list of job opportunities for the unemployed.

18. One church in Baltimore, Payne Memorial African Methodist Episcopal Church, hosts "soap-opera luncheons," bringing young women to watch these television programs and then discuss what they saw. Five of the first twenty-five women were inspired to return to college and earn degrees. Others started their own businesses.

19. Public relations. Essential to meeting needs in the community is letting the community know about the ministries your church offers. You might be the friendliest and most loving people in the country, but no one will know about it in your community unless

you tell them. Word of mouth is best, but a public relations committee or other such group can make a powerful impact for Jesus Christ.

20. In his book *Conspiracy of Kindness,* Pastor Steve Sjogren writes about the servant evangelism of his church, which includes some of the ideas above, such as the free oil change for single mothers. His church, however, has taken this idea to another level, offering dozens of activities for members of his church to connect with the community by meeting needs. All of their projects are done free of charge. Among many are the following: neighborhood windshield washing, snow removal, feeding parking meters (now illegal in some communities), food delivery to shut-ins, leaf raking, lawn care, soda giveaway, free coffee, balloon giveaway, blood pressure screening, cleaning fireplaces, and several dozen more.[20] The remarkable results of many of these projects include the rapid growth of Vineyard Community Church, Cincinnati, Ohio.

There are many more ways in which a church can practice hospitality toward its community and meet needs in the process, probably so many that they could fill many volumes on the subject. But rather than proliferate these ideas endlessly, we leave the basic idea to the creativity of the individual and turn now to the ways in which several churches have practiced hospitality in their ministries.

Discussion

1. How important was hospitality for the early church?

2. What are the qualities of a hospitable person?

3. What practical ideas especially appeal to you at the personal level? congregational level? community level?

4. How might you provide leadership in offering hospitality at the congregational level? community level?

5. What is the myth of greeters? Do you agree or disagree? What might be done to enable greeters to demonstrate hospitality?

Endnotes

1. Keith D. Wright, "Extending the Welcome Mat," *Evangelism* 10, no. 3 (May 1996): 104–5.
2. Wright, "Extending the Welcome Mat," 104.
3. Edythe Draper, *Draper's Book of Quotations for the Christian World* (Wheaton: Tyndale House, 1992), entry 5957.
4. David M. Gustafson, "Scratch Where They Itch," *Evangelism* 10, no. 4 (August 1996): 135.
5. Herb Miller, ed. "Draw a Circle That Takes Them In," *Net Results* 3 (September 1982): 1.
6. Miller, "Draw a Circle That Takes Them In," 2, 5.
7. Wright, "Extending the Welcome Mat," 105.
8. Wright, "Extending the Welcome Mat," 105–6.
9. Bruce J. Lieske, "Growing in Christian Friendship and Hospitality" (St. Louis: The Board for Evangelism Services, The Lutheran Church—Missouri Synod).
10. Howard Snyder, *The Problem of Wineskins* (Downers Grove, Ill.: InterVarsity Press, 1976), 89–90.
11. Lieske, "Growing in Christian Friendship and Hospitality," 7.
12. Eugene Heideman, "Alone at the After-Worship Coffeepot," *Net Results* 14, no. 2 (February 1993): 23.
13. Joe A. Harding, "Imagination in Ministry," *Net Results* 10, no. 12 (December 1989): 12.
14. Larry Gilbert, "Small Group Evangelism: Using AMEs and RSAs to Reach People for Christ," *Church Growth Institute Newsletter* 1, no. 12, pp. 8–9.

15. Arnell P. C. Arn and Jerry Jamison, " 'Bridge Events' Reach New People in Creative, Unique Ways," *Net Results* 17, no. 12 (December 1996): 28.
16. Richard Roland, "Evangelism Coffees Get Instant Results," *Net Results* 2, no. 11 (August 1981): 3.
17. Miller, "Draw a Circle That Takes Them In," 1.
18. Kenneth Zorn. "Friendship Evangelism." Address at the Great Commission Convocation. St. Louis: KFUO Lutheran Radio, 1984.
19. "What's Next? Highlights from the Drucker-Schaller Forum," *NEXT* 4, no. 1 (January–February 1998): 1.
20. Steven Sjogren, *Conspiracy of Kindness* (Ann Arbor: Servant Publications, 1993), 212–26.

Session 6

Parable Churches

I now considered myself as bound by the laws of hospitality to a people who had treated me with so much expense and magnificence. Jonathan Swift, *Gulliver's Travels*

We've just listed dozens of ideas that churches can use at the congregational level or the community level to practice hospitality toward the people in their area. But how does this type of ministry look in the local church, when the church intentionally practices hospitality? Hospitality just doesn't happen naturally at either the congregational level or the community level. Hospitality at the family level is not necessarily connected to the ministry of the church. Consequently, at the congregational level someone, usually a staff person, needs to oversee the ministry, remaining in contact with lay people. This staff person will recruit members of the congregation for hospitality evangelism, hold training meetings, handle the troubleshooting, carry out publicity, and maintain contact so as to keep this ministry in the forefront of the people who have volunteered to open their homes to their unbelieving neighbors.

My recommendation would be for a staff person to begin to publicize a training meeting for all people in the congregation who would love to reach out but feel incapable of talking about their faith. Naturally, those who are comfortable talking about Jesus Christ can come too, but the first group needs more attention.

At the training meeting, the leader would take participants through a Bible study that covers the five key New Testament passages, as well as portions of the ministry of Jesus, especially Luke 14:12–14 and Matthew 25:35–40. Then, utilizing the concept of the three levels of hospitality, explain that the church wants to begin a ministry of hospitality at all three levels, but the leader will work formally only with the congregational and community levels. After presenting many of the options for implementation, the leader will ask participants to indicate on a piece of paper those areas of ministry in which they would like to be involved and the level or lev-

81

els of their involvement. Perhaps they would like to begin a need-meeting ministry that involves a special skill that they have, such as a mechanic who would like to organize a Car Care Clinic. Perhaps they would like to begin a home Bible study, or perhaps they would like to make a commitment to invite a neighbor family to their home every month for the next twelve months.

The staff person records all commitments and begins to keep records. He or she keeps in contact with all those who signed up, either through regular, monthly meetings, where people report the events of the past month, through telephone calls to each person, through e-mail messages, through visits in the homes, or through a variety of these methods.

In the pages that follow, several pastors or lay leaders write about their churches. They explain the hospitality outreach of their church. These leaders come from a variety of denominations, different parts of the country, and a wide variety of ministry styles.

Elmbrook Church, Waukesha County, Wisconsin, is a non-denominational church located just west of Milwaukee. Active membership exceeds three thousand adults. Average worship attendance is 5,500 adults. The church is known for its biblical teaching and preaching, small group Bible studies, and extensive lay involvement. Elmbrook has planted seven other churches in the Milwaukee metropolitan area.

Trinity Lutheran Church, Oregon City, Oregon, until recently pastored by Mark Halvorson, was founded in 1921 in one of the oldest communities in the West. It has an average worship attendance of 335 with 250 in Sunday school and Bible study. Three full-time, four part-time, and four volunteer staff serve the congregation. After nearly ten years as senior pastor, Pastor Halvorson recently accepted a call to start new churches in southern Minnesota. Trinity is a member congregation of The Lutheran Church—Missouri Synod.

Colonial Presbyterian Church, a 2,100 member congregation in **Kansas City, Missouri,** has a national reputation as a large and vibrant church with a wide variety of programs. In the community, Colonial is looked upon as a citywide leader, which hosts many gatherings due to its convenient location and large facilities. Colonial is unashamedly an evangelistic church!

Crystal Evangelical Free Church, New Hope, Minnesota, is a rapidly growing congregation of more than 3,000 members, with a strong ministry to children, youth, and families throughout metropolitan Minneapolis, Minnesota. A staff of twelve ministers and sixty other support staff serve the church. Founded in 1949, Crystal Evangelical Free Church reaches out to ethnic communities locally and internationally.

Neil Atkinson of **Colorado Springs, Colorado,** is president of **Next! Leadership Foundation,** an organization founded to help individuals and organizations discover, understand, and utilize what they do best. He has extensive background and experience with Young Life, focusing especially on leadership development.

Glasgow Reformed Presbyterian Church, Bear, Delaware, began in the mid-1980s with thirty-five people and now worships 1,100, all in one service. The church works with an Ephesians 4 approach, seeking to equip the body of Christ for service. Glasgow uses a hub-and-spokes model, with worship at the hub and a strong house-church ministry as the spokes. Fifty percent of worshipers participate in the house-church ministry, the primary evangelism and caretaking arm of the church.

First Baptist Church, Leesburg, Florida, has averaged more than 300 Baptisms a year over the last seven years. Through identifying unmet needs in the community and then constructing ministries to meet those needs in the name of Christ, the church has found numerous opportunities to share the Gospel. As a result, First Baptist, which worships more than a thousand on a weekend, has been in the top one-half of one percent of all Southern Baptist Convention churches in evangelism. Their motto is "Meeting needs, sharing Christ."

Elmbrook Church
Waukesha County, Wisconsin

Rev. Richard Gorski

In February 1998, Elmbrook Church celebrated its fortieth anniversary. Over those forty years the membership of the church has grown from five families to more than three thousand people. Average attendance at the three weekend services is 5,500 adults, and the church's mailing list contains 15,000 names. All of this growth has taken place without ever conducting a demographic study of the area, developing a marketing plan, carrying out any church-wide evangelistic campaigns, or, until the last five years, having anyone on the church staff with primary responsibility for evangelism and outreach. The growth has taken place because each member of Elmbrook Church has taken seriously the responsibility to reach out to friends and neighbors with the Gospel of Jesus Christ. This vision for growth is communicated to the membership of the church frequently. Many people put this vision into practice in their own homes through a variety of formal and informal events.

In fact, our belief is that evangelistic programs that feature a single presentation of the Gospel in a formal church setting have become minimally effective. That is not to say that there is no place for such presentations, or that the Holy Spirit cannot use them to bring people into the kingdom with a flash of insight. We simply recognize one of the new realities of a post-Christian society. When dealing with people in such a society, a single presentation of the Gospel rarely serves to provide a person with enough information about the Gospel to trust in Christ. A person with little understanding of the Bible usually needs to be able to ask questions and to hear the Gospel explained several times before trusting in Christ. Furthermore, in an increasingly suspicious society characterized by telemarketing and infomercials, a presentation of the Gospel by a stranger rarely gets past questions of motivation. The church is not exempt from such questions. People believe that churches are not interested in them as persons, but only as membership statistics or as checkbooks. *Our experience is that truly effective presentations of the Gospel are those that are made in the context of a relationship which will provide multiple opportunities to talk about Christ.* Once again, many of our members find that opening their homes to friends and neighbors is the best way to accomplish these goals.

We view our role as a local church to be helping our members relate to the people with whom they are in contact every day. Specifically, we view our role as equipping and motivating our members for outreach and providing an environment for outreach to take place. We equip people through Sunday morning classes which train people in personal evangelism and through seminars designed to prepare our members to take part in our formal outreach programs. We motivate people to be involved in outreach by devoting an entire week of our twelve week membership class to the topic and by inviting those who are reaching out and those who have been reached to talk about their experiences as part of our worship services. These testimonies are intended to communicate that outreach is everyone's responsibility, and that God can use anyone who is willing. Finally, we provide an environment for outreach by establishing some specific programs designed to help people use their homes for outreach. Some people find the structure of these formal programs to be very helpful. Others prefer to develop their own, informal methods. Through all these means God is using the hospitality of the people of Elmbrook Church to reach out to their friends and neighbors.

Formal Programs

Over the years we have organized a number of different programs at Elmbrook to help people practice hospitality. These programs have proven successful in their own right and also have served to stimulate the creative thinking of the people who have developed their own ideas for evangelism in their homes.

Neighborhood Bible Clubs are Elmbrook's version of a traditional vacation Bible school taken into people's homes. Dozens of Elmbrook members volunteer to host these weeklong clubs in their homes and yards each summer. The hosts are not required to lead or teach the club. The hosts use their ability to be hospitable. Other adults volunteer to use their gifts of teaching, music, and art. Out of all these volunteers, teams are put together to lead the group at each host's home. The host is primarily responsible to invite the children living in that neighborhood to the club. Of course, personal invitations are always the most effective. More than half of the children who attend these clubs are not from Elmbrook Church.

Many of these clubs make an effort to reach out beyond the children who come to the families of the children. One of the groups hosted a Friday evening closing program for the children and their families at the home where the club met. After the children had recited their verses and sung their songs, one of the adult leaders of the club told the parents what Christ means to him. Several of the parents who attended that closing program are now attending a weekly Bible study sponsored by Elmbrook.

Other groups have taken the principles of the Neighborhood Bible Clubs and applied them in other creative ways. Several people have hosted a *Birthday Party for Jesus* in their homes around Christmas. Others have hosted Valentine's Day parties for the children in their neighborhoods. At these parties the children learn about God's love for them. The success of these programs affirms that children, like adults, respond most positively to the Gospel when someone takes a personal interest in them.

Christmas Teas are outreach events sponsored by our Women's Ministry. A woman who hosts a Christmas Tea personally invites her neighbors to attend, decorates her home, and often provides special or traditional Christmas pastries. Other women prepare a program that includes a presentation of the Gospel in a fashion appropriate to the season. After welcoming her guests and allowing everyone time to mingle, the host introduces the special Christmas program. The program, often including music, personal testimony, and a short talk about the real meaning of Christmas, is usually put together by people other than the host. Initially, the Elmbrook Women's Ministry coordinated these teas, but over the years people have taken it upon themselves to organize them. People now look forward to serving each year in the way they are gifted.

Finally, despite our emphasis on personal outreach rather than church-wide events, *major events* such as musical and dramatic productions and concerts play a role in our outreach. However, even these major events are planned not as ends in themselves, but as providing opportunities for people to use hospitality for outreach. Our intention is not that people will merely buy tickets for their friends and neighbors and send them to an event to hear the Gospel. Our intention is that people will bring their friends and neighbors to the events and host their friends at their homes afterwards. The event easily provides natural opportunities to talk about the spiritual issues the event raised.

Informal Efforts

Just as important as our formal, organized plans are those that people have developed on their own. Some of these ideas are implemented within the context of existing Elmbrook ministries. Others are developed with friends and family or individually.

One of Elmbrook's strengths is its network of more than one hundred *weekly small group Bible studies* that meet in homes around the Milwaukee metropolitan area. Many of these groups view the neighborhood in which they meet as their own outreach responsibility. One of these groups took four weeks out of their normal study topic to make a special effort to reach their neighborhood. Because the majority of the families in their neighborhood had teenage children, they chose to show some videotapes of Dr. James Dobson on parenting teens. Because Dobson's tips on parenting are broadcast on many secular radio stations, people are more likely to attend than if it were advertised as a strictly religious event. (Care must be taken, however, to let people know there will be biblical content. Deception is not an effective means for communicating the Gospel.) The home was full of people, and the subject matter afforded many opportunities for discussion at the Bible study and in the weeks that followed.

Another group used the season of Christmas to host a special event. Every person in the study invited one other person to come on the regular study night to a Christmas party. After the singing of carols and sharing of cookies put everyone at ease, the group sat down together for a brief program. Everyone was asked to relate one Christmas memory or tradition. The group had arranged the seating so that the last person to talk was one of the study members for whom Christmas had been significant in that person coming to faith in Christ. One of the guests that evening had only recently arrived in the United States from India. He had had no previous contact with Christianity. That night was the beginning of a series of conversations with the person who had invited him which eventually led to his coming to faith.

Outside the context of existing ministry groups, many couples and individuals host dinner parties in their home designed for outreach. At these parties there is no formal program, but the Christians at the party are relied on to strike up conversations with the other guests which may lead to spiritual discussion. We have learned that several keys make this an effective strategy. First, these parties seem to work best with an equal number of Christians and other guests. Second, be sure that your Christian guests will be gracious in this social setting. All it takes is one Christian denouncing the government or the public school system or espousing a particular end-times scenario to ensure that the party will have the opposite effect from that intended. Finally, you must decide what to do with the bottle of wine some of your guests might bring in accord with social customs. We tell people they have three options: to accept it graciously and set it aside unopened, to open it and offer some to the guests, or to open it and have some (presumably after offering some to the guests). The one response which is definitely not acceptable is to announce that you are a Christian and therefore would never even consider committing the horrible sin of having a drink.

Finally, it does not take a group to practice hospitality. Many individuals quietly offer hospitality to those around them. One woman made it a practice to leave baked goods and a welcome note for every newcomer to her apartment building. A casual relationship that began with one particular newcomer bore fruit when the newcomer's mother died and she asked the Elmbrook member what she believed about heaven. Another Elmbrook couple met a first-time visitor to the church one Sunday morning. They asked the visitor to come to their home for dinner one day. The visitor asked, "When?" They responded, "How about in two hours?" That visitor is actively involved in the church today—because two people exercised hospitality.

So practice hospitality. Do it in the context of a relationship. Do it formally and informally, in the home or at the church, over a meal or in another way, as an individual or as a group, on a regular basis or occasionally or seasonally. But "practice *hospitality*" (Romans 12:13).

Trinity Lutheran Church
Oregon City, Oregon

Rev. Mark Halvorson

An understanding of our setting helps us to appreciate how much God has blessed us. Our entire facility is on three-tenths of one acre on the side of a hill in a nationally registered historic neighborhood. Oregon City is the oldest incorporated city west of the Mississippi and was the termination point of the Oregon Trail. Oregon and Washington are two of the three most unchurched states in the nation. Our building is divided into five different levels, and the rooms are all fairly small and not always easy for the visitor to locate. There is no off-street parking associated with the church. An emphasis on being warm and friendly is especially important because the campus cannot be the focus. Having such a limited facility has encouraged us to make people and the quality of ministry our main focus.

Hospitality has played a very important part in the growth and health of Trinity. By 1988 the church had plateaued at 160 worshipers each Sunday, and the overall membership was growing older. The people were in no way intentionally unfriendly toward strangers, but few had a clear biblical understanding of the role that Christ-centered warmth and hospitality play in growing a healthy church. My first opportunity as the new pastor was to change that. My first task was to search the Scriptures along with the people of Trinity and have God remind us of the real purpose of His church.

One of my first sermon and Bible study series focused on being more loving and friendly as expressions of what we believe. I built the studies around Scripture passages that clearly show us that Christ demonstrated a loving disposition toward people. Hospitality and the role it plays in showing Christ's love to the stranger was highlighted. Through personal, caring contact Jesus showed people that they mattered individually. He loved the stranger and taught it in parables like that of the Good Samaritan. He taught His Father's truths and demonstrated His love for people. Lutheran Christians who know they are loved by Jesus Christ began to understand that they are also called and empowered to love others for Him. Within a few weeks, acts of warmth and love were popping up everywhere! Visitors saw these warm smiles, friendly handshakes, and sincere welcomes. Our church grew by fifty-two in attendance our first year together and has grown ever since. This is not to say that everything has been perfect and our growth uninterrupted; that is not the case. Still, God has blessed Trinity with unity, optimism about the future, and growth.

Concrete ideas and examples accompanied Bible teachings on how each of us can be more caring in action. Christ calls us to be like Him in belief, attitude, and actions. I spent teaching and training time in each of these areas: belief, attitudes, and actions. For many of our members it was the first time they clearly understood how their lives—how we act as well as what we say—matter to God and those to whom He is reaching out. The importance of the laity and their role in evangelism must be understood if any kind of sustained evangelistic action is to take place. Sunday morning is the most obvious place to begin to teach this lifestyle of Christian authenticity.

The people appreciated hearing specific ideas on how to help the visitor feel more welcome. For example, since we have no off-street parking and a very, very small narthex, we talked about not parking directly in front of the main entrance. This area was turned into a drop-off zone, and the members were encouraged not to park on the block in front of the church building. Of course, not everyone followed this advice, but enough did so that the late-arriving visitor regularly found parking near the entrance of the church. Greeters were stationed at the front of the church to welcome everyone, especially guests. They remained there until we were fifteen minutes into the worship. Ushers were trained in hospitality and making the visitor feel welcomed. The most effective resource was John Maxwell's video series *Ushers and Greeters*. Trained and individually motivated elders and leaders would also greet people outside as they approached the front of the sanctuary. No one could get into the worship service at Trinity without being welcomed!

Because of these efforts, visitors immediately sense the warmth and friendliness of the members. This is intentional and a reflection of our primary purpose to be used by God to make disciples who make a difference for Jesus Christ. When I first arrived, I taught and modeled that Christian love was mostly expressed in action. I really do not think that most members understood the powerful influence they could have on visitors and the overall vitality of our church. As we saw how God blessed us with health, unity, and growth, we developed more ways to share the love of Christ with those who needed Him. Once the information was presented to the people of Trinity, they were motivated to be a warm, welcoming church.

Other aspects of warmth we intentionally worked on as a congregation were laughter, genuine smiles, and sincere verbal greetings. Asking for and sharing names, nametags, and appropriate touching were also taught and modeled. Appropriate touching means a firm handshake, grasping someone's hand with both of your hands, or gently greeting someone by taking their hand and their arm above the elbow. These are simple, common sense ways of showing people you are glad that they are present. One of the favorite phrases I used in teaching these simple greeting techniques was this: "I can teach the words and methods, but it is up to you to provide the sincerity!" Yes, these are all simple things, and no techniques cause the church to grow. Only God can grow His church, yet somehow genuine warmth makes people more receptive to hearing about Jesus Christ. This is all part of being a good steward!

Over the years we have expanded the impact of loving the stranger for Christ as we intentionally recruited and trained visitation teams, greeters, Stephen ministers, and TLC care groups. My goal was to equip more believers to demonstrate Christlike service, warmth, and Christian care giving. The assimilation team and Home Bible Fellowship leaders were encouraged to model hospitality. The pastor who preceded me, Lornell Ruthenbeck, was called back to minister to the seniors, and he, in turn, organized and trained them to reach out to visitors from their generation. In one year this ministry team of caregivers sent over 300 cards, made more than 450 phone calls, and performed 150 acts of kindness such as helping a widow with home repairs. All of the staff we have added in recent years shows that loving people is a significant way demonstrating our faith in Jesus Christ. These key leaders are doing a great job of developing their areas of ministry around service and outreach. These praying servants and the great work they are doing are the most important factors in what God is doing at Trinity. I deeply love and appreciate them.

Two examples are our preschool and youth ministries. Our preschool teacher, Mrs. Suzanne Walters, is a very loving person. She loves children, and the parents of these youngsters strongly sense care for their children. She is especially attentive to the needs of the unchurched families who have children in attendance. She asks parents questions and seeks to get to know them on a personal level. Christ shines through her! Because of her warmth and the quality program she has developed, our morning preschool sessions are full. This last year we expanded to an afternoon session.

Our youth leader, Larry Deyoe, shares many of the same traits as Mrs. Walters. He greets the youth individually as they enter the youth room. He has made this room warm and inviting so that when the youth enter, they feel that this is an environment that is oriented toward them. Weekly he takes youth out to lunch or invites them to his home. One day a week he disc jockeys at a local Christian radio station, and through that ministry has met numerous Christian artists. Through that work he has been able to secure autographed posters for our youth room, and a few of the musicians have even met with our youth personally. Simple things like these have impressed our youth and greatly strengthened the ministry.

On Sunday mornings I understand the important role the senior pastor has in setting the tone for the worship service. Creating an atmosphere of love is critical, as I try to bring an appropriate balance of reverence and joy. Tasteful humor and an upbeat approach are important in making people feel welcome and ready to worship Christ. Studies have clearly shown that the authenticity and warmth of the person leading the worship service are what the visitor notices most. It really is important that I am genuinely caring, show joy in their presence, and indicate that I firmly believe what I am preaching and teaching. My sincerity and authenticity will be a positive influence in their being more willing to listen to the Savior behind the messenger and the message. If the pastor is not demonstrating these characteristics of authenticity, then it will be more of a challenge for the people to exude friendliness to the visitor and to one another. The pastor must not only be the loving leader but the leading lover of souls!

Colonial Presbyterian Church
Kansas City, Missouri

Rev. Keith Wright

One of our members approached me several years ago and said, "Pastor Keith, you and the other ministers continually challenge us to reach out to our unchurched neighbors. But I don't even know my neighbors! How do I get to know them?" The question really hit home. All along I had assumed that people knew how to establish relationships with their neighbors, but we needed to educate our congregation on how to build friendships with those who live around them. Each year in our newsletter we publish a list of ways that our members can build relationships in their neighborhoods. The following ideas were printed in last year's article:

Okay. You're convinced you should reach out to your neighbors in Christian love. What's stopping you? The "perfect" moment hasn't arrived yet? No more excuses! Here are some ways to develop friendships with neighbors all year long. Some ideas will lead to a block party, others to one-on-one friendships, and still others to service. These ideas will get you started—and once relationships are established, you might just get to share your faith!

January—Super Bowl Party. Invite a group over to watch the big game. Provide lots of munchies. Root for your favorite team!

February—Gift Basket Clinic. If you're "artsy," why not teach your neighbors how to put together a romantic gift for that someone special in their life?

March—Walking Club. Organize scheduled treks around the neighborhood. Walk and talk. Notice what's happening on your block. The arrival of new babies, illnesses, and deaths provide windows for further outreach.

April—Progressive Dinner. Because of short distances, neighborhoods are perfect venues for progressive dinners. Start with appetizers at one house, salad at the next, and so on. Conclude with dessert and a game.

May—Annual Scraping of the Grills. Around Memorial Day get permission to block off your street. Inaugurate summer with a parade of barbecues. "Grill out" together.

June—Croquet Party. There's nothing like a croquet match to while away a summer evening. Set up the wickets, call some neighbors, and play a leisurely match.

July—Ice Cream Social. This past summer, some of my friends hosted an ice cream social. Seventy-five neighbors joined in the camaraderie that warm summer evening!

August—House-Sitting. When vacation rolls around, neighbors often need someone to feed the pets, water the plants, and pick up the mail. How about serving your neighbors while they're away?

September—Perennial Swap. Many landscape their yards with perennials—which can be "split" and replanted.

October—Halloween Fun House. This past Halloween I walked by a house with a sign out front—"Halloween Carnival, All Friendly Creatures Welcome." Feeling friendly, I ventured in. I found a few games, great food, and several families enjoying a fun alternative to trick-or-treating. My treat was hanging out with neighbors.

November—Leaf Cleanup. Autumn is cleanup time—and brings people out into their yards. Strike up conversations and be friendly. Serve a neighbor by raking and bagging that person's leaves.

December—Christmas Cookie Exchange. Each guest brings four to six dozen cookies. After a fun evening together, everyone swaps cookies and takes home a wonderful assortment of goodies.

We also encourage our members to open their homes for evangelistic purposes. The following ideas are the most popular among our membership:

Dinner for Eight. Eight people gather for dinner, fellowship, and fun. By including a few non-Christians, new relationships often emerge—leading to invitations to adult Sunday school classes, worship services, and special church events where the Gospel is presented.

Fondue Party. Who can resist chocolate? A group is invited over for "Fondue and a Discussion of the Christian Faith." The group enjoys dessert and socializing together. Then a spiritually mature person makes a ten-minute presentation on the relevancy of a relationship with Christ. An open discussion time follows for guests to ask questions. A group of twenty people works best, half non-Christians. Variations on this theme include evangelistic barbecues, coffee-tasting parties, or burrito bars.

Literary Society. Reading groups have gained popularity in our congregation over the past few years. These literary societies intentionally include seekers. They gather monthly in a living room to discuss, debate, and dissect a selected reading. Both Christian and secular authors are chosen. Whatever work is chosen, believers contribute a Christian perspective to the discussion. An atmosphere of intellectual honesty is encouraged, where believers and nonbelievers alike can stretch their thinking.

Youth House. Teenagers love to just hang out. They appreciate homes where they are welcomed, where a wholesome atmosphere provides a place for friendships, and where adults are involved and listen. Several families in our church have established an open-door policy and have communicated that policy to the kids in our youth group.

Personal Coaching. We have discovered that providing personal coaching is an effective means of helping our members to be more evangelistic. One way we have done this is by using Neil Atkinson as an evangelism coach. Neil served as a Young Life regional director for more than twenty-five years. Neil comes to Kansas City each quarter and meets with a select group of fifteen to twenty people who are trying to hone their evangelism skills. The small-group setting and one-on-one interaction with Neil allow the participants to grow in their abilities to establish relationships with nonbelievers, to invite them into their homes, and to guide their friends in the process of entering into a relationship with Christ. This approach has taken a lot of the fear out of personal evangelism.

We have provided coaching of a different sort through our adult Sunday school classes. Several classes have viewed the video series

Becoming a Contagious Christian, produced by Willow Creek Community Church. Although this video series focuses on lifestyle evangelism, most of the techniques can be implemented in homes. Our adult Sunday school classes have served as peer coaches to one another as they endeavor to implement the principles of this video series.

Jesus Video Project. Colonial Presbyterian Church has been at the forefront of a citywide evangelistic effort in conjunction with the *Jesus* Video Project—a ministry of Campus Crusade for Christ. Its goal is to place a *Jesus* video into every home in America. Members of our congregation are encouraged to build relationships with their neighbors through some of the methods listed above. Then, during the Christmas season, our members deliver a gift-wrapped copy of the *Jesus* video, along with a plate of cookies to their neighbors. Over 4,000 copies of the *Jesus* video were distributed by our membership the past two Christmases.

Neighborhood Households of Prayer/Community Groups. Colonial's Small Group Ministry and Prayer Ministry are working together to establish a neighborhood household of prayer in every subdivision in Kansas City. Church members volunteer their homes as the designated prayer households in their neighborhoods. Door hangers are placed at each house in the neighborhood stating when the prayer group meets. There is also space for prayer requests to be written on the door hanger, which can be rehung on the door for collection. These prayer requests are prayed for during the regular meetings of the neighborhood prayer groups. Our desire is for a particular home to develop a reputation as the place where Christians gather to pray because they care about the neighborhood's needs. Many have been drawn into these prayer meetings because of answered prayer.

Recently, we added another dimension to this ministry by hosting twice monthly Community Groups in these same neighborhoods. The purpose of the Community Groups is to provide a nonthreatening forum for the neighbors to drop by. While the focus of the prayer meeting is on prayer, the focus of Community Groups is upon fellowship. We have found that new residents, in particular, are responsive to an invitation to drop by to meet others in the neighborhood (who happen to be Christians). Once relationships are established, we start seeing these individuals getting involved in other church programs.

Colonial Presbyterian has built outreach into its ministry mentality, and much of it expresses itself in a variety of ways through the building of relationships, especially in hospitable situations.

Crystal Evangelical Free Church New Hope, Minnesota

Rev. Stephen Goold

A number of people and informal ministries at Crystal Evangelical Free Church (CEFC) in suburban Minneapolis, Minnesota, focus on hospitality as the main expression of their heart for ministry. These expressions of hospitality are clearly divided into two channels of love: (1) hospitality toward unbelievers and (2) hospitality toward believers.

Senior Pastor Stephen Goold encourages various members of the Crystal Evangelical Free Church family to utilize their homes as warm, accepting places to introduce their non-Christian friends and acquaintances to God's love, the Bible, and Jesus Christ. One of the most obvious groupings of acquaintances is one's neighbors. Barry and Teresa Peterson are one couple committed to intentional hospitality with neighbors.

Hospitality with Neighbors. Barry and Teresa were the second of thirty families to move into a new subdivision in Plymouth, Minnesota. With every new house that was completed, the Petersons made a point to welcome personally each new homeowner that moved into the neighborhood. They took the newcomers food, told them about the other neighbors, and stressed how friendly all the neighbors were and how much they would enjoy living in the Plymouth neighborhood. That became a self-fulfilling prophecy. Since everyone expected everyone else to be friendly, they themselves acted friendly and outgoing too.

The Petersons have conducted apologetic presentations in their home, as well as couples' Bible studies with neighbors. They have hosted the Fourth of July block party for the last three years. They also have initiated deck parties in the summer, "common backyard" parties (about ten of the houses open up to a common backyard), and Christmas brunches for the wives. Several neighbors have come to faith in Christ as Savior. A highlight several years ago was that six neighborhood families watched the *Jesus* video that Teresa gave them. Neighbors enjoy each other and love living where they do. The Petersons have made a difference in their neighborhood.

Hospitality with Internationals. Dr. Lance Haseltine is a physician, and during 1997 he invited a pharmacy graduate student from China to his home in Corcoran, Minnesota, many times in order to build a friendship with him. The University of Minnesota has more than one thousand Chinese students, mostly graduate and postgraduate scholars, arguably the largest concentration of Chinese students anywhere outside of China. This has presented tremendous ministry opportunities for people like Lance and Brenda Haseltine to show love to internationals who really crave friendships with Americans.

Lance's pharmacist friend came to faith in Jesus Christ in November 1997 because Lance loved him until he asked him why. The Chinese student married another Chinese graduate student in December 1997, and Lance is now discipling both of them. In March, Lance is planning to visit China to lecture in Beijing universities, to interact with Chinese students who want to practice their English and get to know an American physician, and to learn more about Chinese history and culture. Lance is planning to take eleven-year-old Kara, the oldest of his five children, with him to China. Kara is a member of the junior Bible quiz team, and she is already learning firsthand the importance of friendship hospitality. Perhaps God will call her to work in China in the future!

Other members of the Crystal Evangelical Free Church family open up their homes to strangers or to other Christians, especially missionaries. CEFC as a whole and individuals within the church are committed to this ministry of hospitality.

Hospitality House for Missionaries and Guests. In 1997 the elders of CEFC were led by God to purchase a beautiful four-bedroom house located adjacent to the church's parking lot. It has been named the Friendship House. On the weekend this purchase was to be announced to the whole congregation, a member of the church gave Pastor Steve Goold a check for the full price of the house, plus an additional large gift for any repairs or renovations needed. The whole church rallied around this summer project, and by early fall the house had a new roof and deck, was fully furnished by gifts from church members, and was ready to house its first occupants. Missionaries Ken and Ginny McMillan and their children, who had lost all their worldly goods through a recent evacuation from Zaire,

97

are now enjoying a safe haven—the Friendship House, Crystal Evangelical Free Church's corporate commitment to hospitality.

Hospitality for Missionaries. Pastor Monroe Brewer is the global ministries pastor for CEFC. His wife, Joan, has demonstrated hospitality as a main focus of her ministry. Over their twenty-seven years of ministry, the Brewers have hosted in their home representatives—national leaders and missionaries—from more than eighty countries. A number of nationals, both singles (e.g., Singaporeans, French, Eritreans) and couples (e.g., Brazilians), have lived with them for months. Even a family of four from Kenya lived with them for nearly four months. But most come for a few weeks or a few days. It is a tremendous encouragement for missionaries to be able to connect so personally and deeply with Americans committed to them and to their work.

In summary, the ministry of hospitality, thought by many to be a dying art among Christians, is still burning brightly in many Minnesota homes. For some, the motive for hospitality is a compassion that expresses itself in the desire that neighbors or acquaintances may be saved. For others, the motive for hospitality is encouragement, that those working for Christ in hard places around the world will feel important and appreciated. Whatever one's motive, it is a crucial but neglected ministry—one in which everyone can participate in one way or another. At Crystal Evangelical Free Church in Minneapolis, "home is where it's at!"

Next! Leadership Foundation Colorado Springs, Colorado

Neil Atkinson

Nine of us were gathered at our table. Of the seven who were not evangelicals, only two had any sympathy for the faith. Several were openly hostile and ready to do battle. Others just waited.

Dinner was served. Since it was prepared and served by the male evangelical, the feminist contingent was caught somewhat off guard. Nonetheless the atmosphere was politely tense. But Margie and I had been there before. We knew that the excessive intellectual chatter was just a means of jockeying for position. We also knew that if we applied biblical principles of hospitality, the tension would ease. It did.

How? First you must understand that a good part of the genius of our marriage is my wife, Margie. She is a petite babe who is also analytical, academic, and the only person in the world that could have made Mother Teresa look mean. In addition to that resource, we have practiced intentional hospitality through our marriage.

That simply means that it is up to us to create an atmosphere warm enough for people to emerge from their protective shells. There is no magic. It is not hard. It simply applied love. It is a proactive stance, not a reactive flinch. It means understanding that the people in our home, though opposed to the faith, are not our enemies, but individuals who need to see and hear the truth.

It means forgetting ourselves and focusing on our guests. As John Maxwell said, "There are two kinds of people in the world: *'Here I am, how am I doing?'* and 'There *you* are, how are *you* doing?' All that it takes to create a safe environment is to be a "there you are" person.

This practical theology is very easy to learn and not that difficult to put into practice. Hundreds have grasped and applied the principle. Like any skill, it gets better the more we use it. Here is the key: use basic journalism questions to start conversations, that is, who, what, when, how, where, and why. You can talk with anyone by continuing to use questions about them, for example, where did you two meet, what degree did you earn, what motivated you to go into your current career, and so on.

Many of us are intimidated by people who are too wealthy, too talented, too intellectual, too attractive, too poor, too atheistic. We perhaps feel that we do not measure up and that conversation with such people would be difficult. Not true. Henrietta Mears once said, "Treat everybody as if they wore a sign that said, 'I am lonely and in need of a friend,' and you won't miss by far." Focusing on other people allows us to forget what we don't have and presents them with a gracious example of caring. This caring allows the warmth of genuine hospitality to melt a difficult atmosphere. Back to the story!

It's funny what a meal will do to a group of people. Good food, good wine (but not too much!), and good conversation centering on genuine care and respect for each person carried away most of the initial unease. As dessert was served, I guided the conversation to talking about our spiritual histories. The guests were only too eager to share.

The fundamental principle involved here is that we must find out the spiritual history of nonbelieving adults in order to care for them in terms they understand.

Most stories were helpful in providing information for understanding the people and how they had arrived at their current spiritual condition. Betty's story stood out:

> I was raised in the Methodist Church for eighteen years and I really liked it. Until, that is, the day my pastor raped me. Then I joined a fundamentalist church, and I had to stand in front of them when I joined and tell them all of my sins. Later they threw me out. *And,* you know, all I wanted to do was love Jesus.

The table was very silent after hearing that brief, painful description. I mentioned how embarrassed I was for the actions of the church and that I hurt deeply for the spiritual and physical abuse she had gone through. That small attempt at reconciliation was enough. Rather than rail at the church, people were more inclined to be open and hospitable themselves. They stayed three hours and did not want to leave.

Group hospitality can easily lead to individual hospitality. Remember that we all are, as Garrison Keillor so eloquently states, "greedy monsters for a drop of love." If the group is cared for and nurtured through good hospitality, there will be a connection of some sort, a positive chemical reaction with one or two of the guests. This could lead to intentional efforts to form relationships by doing things together that are mutually enjoyable, such as going out for lunch, playing golf, visiting art museums, attending concerts or sporting events.

During these individual times we only need to stay on the track of "There *you* are, how are *you* doing." We can offer genuine concern, and we can do it for a long period of time. The process of caring is the most important part of hospitality. Hit and run does not work. If we offer a one-time shot, the chances are that people will see behind the intentions: they were a project. What can happen over months and years of caring for someone in terms they understand and not demanding anything from them?

Curt was a successful professional in Chicago. He moved to California, where he became very successful. But then he fell on hard times, very hard times. He lost almost everything. I met him through a mutual acquaintance, and we had positive chemistry and started doing things together. We drank lots of coffee, skied often, played golf some, and my wife and I had his family over for dinner.

One morning he called and asked if we could go to lunch. He

was very shaken. The deal he was counting on to put him back on track had fallen through. For two hours he let it out—all the pain, frustration, and hurt. I listened.

At the end of the time, I asked if I could pray for him. (I know, how creative on my part. But remember, I had heard his spiritual story, knew what he could take, and I didn't know what else to do!) He said, "Sure," and got up to leave. I stopped him and said, "I mean now." He was shocked, but he said, "Go ahead," and he bowed his head. I prayed something, said "amen," and looked up to see Curt crying.

He said, "Two things: you are only the third man in my life who has seen me cry, and second, what I am crying about has nothing to do with what we have talked about for two hours" (i.e., his business failure). I then asked him why he was crying. He said very simply, "Because someone cares."

To make a long story short, in a manner of weeks Curt trusted Christ and has been growing in Him ever since.

Intentional, process hospitality—it can make someone's day and maybe affect their life for eternity.

Glasgow Reformed Presbyterian Church Bear, Delaware

Robert M. Horton

Dr. Douglas Perkins, Glasgow Reformed Presbyterian Church associate pastor, and his wife, Pam, have adopted a motto defining Christian hospitality as an attitude of gratitude. Knowing that Christ reached out to influence their hearts when in fact their hearts were estranged from Him, in a Christlike manner, they have extended Christian hospitality to those who are estranged in their community: foreign students.

They shared a number of illustrations from their lives revealing the heartfelt impact of hospitality. While growing up in Massachusetts, Doug had a paper route. One couple stood out above all the rest to that young, unregenerate Yankee teenager. When others would just leave their payment in an envelope taped to their door or stand there yawning in their bathrobe and hand it to him through a narrowly opened doorway, Mr. and Mrs. Gile would open their door wide and invite him in for a pancake breakfast. They gave him gifts on special occasions and were always the biggest tippers. They lived an attitude of gratitude for what Christ had done for them. They extended Christ's love and ultimately the Gospel of grace to that boy who would later come to see them as his welcomers to the heavenly banquet table of Christ. Hospitality pancakes helped usher Doug into God's kingdom! The moral of this story is to look for opportunities with people who regularly enter your sphere of influence, and seek creative ways to influence them for Christ.

Doug also tells of how a Maryland attorney and his wife were compelled by Christ's love to open the door of their home on Friday nights to the town's teens. The second time they did this, a young, unregenerate pagan and a bunch of his buddies got into a fight in the attorney's living room. The youth threw his opponent through the window. It seems that the price of opening their front door was an unorthodox opening of their bay window! Later, however, that young man came to Christ. He has since gone into the ministry and is a youth pastor for the church of the attorney with bay-window air conditioning! Here's a couple who was willing to pay a price to participate in propagating God's grace to others.

Do you have this attitude of gratitude? If not but you'd like to have it, pray for God to grant it. Try praying by paraphrasing God's Scripture back to Him. I'll illustrate that here:

"For the LORD your God is God of gods and Lord of lords, the great God, mighty and awesome, *who shows no partiality* and accepts no bribes" (Deuteronomy 10:17).

Lord, I thank You that You showed no partiality against me and my sin, but You called me unto You through the love shown to me by Your people.

"He defends the cause of the fatherless and the widow, and *loves the alien,* giving him food and clothing" (Deuteronomy 10:18).

Lord, You came to my rescue and caused me to see my spiritual bankruptcy; when I was treating You as an enemy, You showed me Your love and mercy in Christ.

"And *you are to love those who are aliens,* for you yourselves were aliens in Egypt" (Deuteronomy 10:19).

Lord, help me to love those who are now alienated from You. For just as You led me out of my Egypt, use me to lead others out from the bondage of their sin.

"Fear the LORD your God and serve Him. Hold fast to Him and take your oaths in His name" (Deuteronomy 10:20).

Lord, help each of us to revere Your holy name. May we cling to Your promises, may we live out an oath of allegiance to Your name, may we minister to others as You have ministered to us.

"He is your praise; He is your God, who performed for you those great and awesome wonders you saw with your own eyes" (Deuteronomy 10:21).

Lord, may we praise You not only with our lips, but also with our lives. Help us be living letters of Your love. We look forward to seeing Your great and awesome wonders as You touch the hearts of those we seek to serve with Christlike love. Cultivate that attitude of gratitude in us—to Your glory. Amen.

Doug and Pam tell how Romans 12 speaks clearly about the prerequisites of being godly as we are in fact hospitable: verse 1: live sacrificially; verse 2: don't follow the world's example; verse 3: humbly regard others above your own self-importance; verses 4 and 5: work in concert with other believers; verses 6–8: employ your spiritual gifts; verses 9–12: be sincere, loving, devoted, fervent, joyful, patient, and faithful in prayer. Finally, having put off sinful attitudes and put on the attributes listed in verses 1–12, we will be ready to glorify God by being faithful to verses 13 and 14: "Share with God's people who are in need. *Practice hospitality.* Bless those who persecute you; bless and do not curse." Note well: hospitality is a command, not a gift!

Be aware, however, that entertaining is not hospitality. Entertaining is seeking to impress. Gourmet cooking, using your house and home as a showplace, that's Martha Stewart. Entertaining seeks to bring glory to you or your possessions and material accomplishments. Hospitality seeks God's glory. Hospitality is ministering that proclaims, "This is not my home; it's God's home." It's done without thought of a return compliment, without motive except the Savior being seen by those who need Him. This is not easy. For example, Doug and Pam invited a half dozen couples to come to their home after attending a Christmas production at the church. The kids drifted down the hall toward the toys, and the parents gravitated toward the living room. The clamor from the kids quieted abruptly. Pam sensed something was amiss and rushed to investigate. One of her three young boys was buried under a mass of pillows and older boys. Now it wasn't a life-threatening situation, but a rescue was definitely in order. This has caused the Perkins to pray fervently over such gatherings and to pray more diligently for these neighbors when they pass by their homes. The Perkins boys also have been led to pray for those youngsters. Since then, some have even joined their backyard Bible club! This confirms 1 Peter 4:8–9, where we are instructed how to stand up for Christ when under persecution for doing good: "Above all, love each other deeply, because love covers over a multitude of sins. *Offer hospitality to one another without grumbling.*" In obedience to Christ, rather than grumbling over this event, they extended themselves even further with prayer and outreach to the families of these boys. God is still at work, in and through the obedience of the whole Perkins family.

One final illustration comes from these ambassadors for Christ. They've traditionally celebrated Christmas at home and traveled the day after to distant relatives. This year, they announced to their three boys that on Christmas Day, they'd be having some international students over for brunch. Two of their boys protested saying, "But Mom, Christmas is a private family thing. We don't want these guys over!" Pam corrected them saying, "Oh, but you're both wrong. Our home belongs to God. Christmas belongs to the Lord. How can we say it's not for these students that don't yet know Christ? How do we know that one of them won't become a Christian?" The boys relented. On Christmas Day, in spite of Pam being sick the night before and not feeling like preparing to feed eight to ten guests, the doorbell rang early and she warmed up some meatballs and leftovers. They enjoyed the simple fixin's and then played some parlor games. After sharing a brief story on the real meaning of Christmas, they stepped outside into Delaware's mild Christmas weather and shot a few hoops. Players represented China, Africa, Lithuania, and the United States and ranged in height from four feet ten inches to six feet ten inches. It made for quite an interesting game. At the end of the day, the Perkins boys declared, "Mom and Dad, this was the best Christmas ever!"

Another aspect of our church's outreach through hospitality is the house-church ministry. Greg and Sally Martin, one couple active in our house-church ministry, have lived a lifestyle that mirrors the concern of Christ for the Samaritan woman. Recently, Greg and Sally bought a new home for their growing family. Like for many of us, their new home was larger than their previous one. Their hearts were larger too. As well as providing more room for their family, they also planned to entertain guests, to open their home to others as a means of ministry so that they might introduce others to the Word of life.

Their story actually began before the new house was built. Tom and Karen, close friends of Greg and Sally, had arranged for Shirley, a recently engaged friend, to be a mother's helper for their family. Tom and Karen raved over the benefits of Shirley's help to Karen. Shirley's roommate Nicole also helped out at times when Shirley was unavailable. Before long, Greg and Sally met both young women. Shirley tried to convince Sally to try her services too, but Sally declined because she didn't feel a need for assistance. Shirley wrote her phone number down and put it in Sally's hand. Sally gave half a smile and accepted it even though she thought she wouldn't be needing Shirley's help.

The very next day, Sally received a phone call from her former employer begging her to come back to work. She was flattered but said no because she wanted to be a stay-at-home mom for her two children. Her ex-boss offered to let Sally telecommute. But she still didn't want to work full-time, even if she didn't have to leave her children or her home. So the boss countered with an offer for part-time hours, even saying that she could set her own salary and hours for this part-time venture! Sally talked this over with Greg and took the job.

This time Sally smiled more fully as she remembered Shirley insisting that she take her phone number. Just a phone call later it was all arranged. Shirley would be there for a couple of days each week. Things went very smoothly. Sometimes, Nicole substituted for Shirley as needed, and both became adopted members of these two church families. Both families shared the Gospel with these two young ladies. Just before her wedding, Shirley made a profession of faith! As of the wedding day, Nicole lost her former roommate to a handsome sailor, and the Martins lost Shirley's childcare services. Nicole also needed to make other rooming arrangements. Greg and Sally had just moved into their new home. The guestroom in their new home now had its first occupant, and Nicole became Shirley's replacement. Nicole lived with the family for several months. As time went on, they had several opportunities to discuss spiritual matters with her. Many of their church friends also had a chance to interact with her. She even joined them on a church picnic.

Perhaps you're thinking that soon Nicole also confessed her faith. So far, that's not the case. She has praised Greg and Sally for their graciousness and has been thoroughly exposed to the grace of Christ in their lives. Nicole moved out to take a job in a distant city. She still calls them for counsel and stays in touch with their kids. She even pops in now and then. The last time she did that, Sally's six-year-old daughter, Sue, asked Nicole if she loved Jesus. She dodged the question, but we hope she ultimately won't be able to dodge the living example of Christ shown to her by Greg, Sally, and now Sue.

First Baptist Church Leesburg, Florida

Michael Chute and John Revell

Charlotte Rubush's rendezvous with the Lord, via ministry evangelism, started several years ago when she fled to Florida with her boyfriend and two children to escape prosecution on drug-related felony charges.

Because of continued drug use, she was arrested again and lost custody of her children. Charlotte was released and placed on two years' probation, but she continued to struggle with her addiction. She and her boyfriend found themselves working day labor to pay for their motel and drugs.

"I remember crying myself to sleep every night, not wanting to go on like this, and desperately missing my children," she said.

A friend suggested she seek help from the Women's Care Center at First Baptist Church of Leesburg, but she initially rejected the idea. Yet, as her desperation grew, she soon found herself at the front door of the Women's Care Center.

"I will never forget the sense of peace that I felt while waiting in the living room to meet with the director," Charlotte said. "That feeling was so intense that I knew everything was going to be all right."

Pastor Charles Roesel has a vision for First Baptist Church of Leesburg. He sees a Christian campus with church members so spiritually equipped that anytime someone sets foot on the property, regardless of the need—physical, emotional, or spiritual—it will be met.

For thirteen years now, Roesel has been leading the Leesburg church around the slogan "The Church That Cares." Roesel believes the biblical basis for what he calls ministry evangelism is found in Matthew 25. He says it calls Christians not to a life of ease, but one of sacrifice and service.

To that end, the people of the Leesburg congregation fill more than 1,400 volunteer positions in eighty-two different ministries. The church recently completed its Ministry Village, which includes two new buildings for the church's Rescue Mission for men and its

Women's Shelter. Those two ministries, dating from 1982 and 1989, respectively, were previously operated in houses the church purchased across the street from its main facilities. Additional Ministry Village facilities house the church's Pregnancy Care Center, Children's Rescue Shelter, and Teen Home, as well as the furniture barn, clothing closet, and food pantry.

For nearly fifteen years, the church's Christian Care Center Inc. (CCC)—a nonprofit corporation—has helped thousands of men, women, children, and families get through the trauma of homelessness, poverty, abuse, neglect, abandonment, hunger, and crisis pregnancies. The ministry, which initially operated in old, renovated houses in Leesburg, has been able to expand its facilities and services through the Ministry Village, built on a city-block area on the church campus.

More than one thousand two hundred children have come through the Children's Rescue Shelter. Over one thousand women a year come to the Pregnancy Care Center. Over three hundred men a year are served through the Rescue Mission. More than two hundred women and children have been helped by the Women's Shelter. And the benevolent ministries—furniture barn, clothing closet, and food pantry—assist over five thousand people a year.

"If we're going reach this world for Christ, there are three things that are absolutely imperative," Roesel said. "First, we'll have to be willing to do some new things." For example, he pointed out, the Leesburg church has started a Saturday version of Sunday school that reaches anywhere from two hundred to four hundred people each Saturday.

"Second, we must do the old things unusually well," he said. "When we start doing new things, it seems like we always want to throw out the old." Roesel said his church has gone back to a two-week vacation Bible school, averaging more than two thousand children enrolled each year.

"Third, we must loose the laity," Roesel said. "Our churches today are dying from staff infection. Every time there's a job to do, we feel like we have to hire someone to do it. There are laymen and laywomen by the hundreds eager to do something for the Lord if we will just loose them for the glory of Christ."

Roesel said that through ministry evangelism his church's laity has taken on much of the responsibility for the ministries and "have freed me to preach, pray, and equip the saints for ministry."

Southern Baptist leaders are using First Baptist Church, Leesburg, as a model for ministry evangelism. Roesel has traveled in over thirty states—including Hawaii and Alaska—sharing his ministry evangelism concepts at conferences, seminaries, and churches. He has taught ministry-based evangelism during the North American Mission Board's church growth conferences at both Ridgecrest and Glorieta conference centers. Roesel has even traveled to Canada and the Bahamas to teach ministry evangelism principles there.

The Sunday School Board (SSB) has planned four national ministry conferences each year at the Leesburg church. In addition, SSB personnel will lead four Kingdom Conferences across the nation each year that will tie into ministry-based evangelism.

"People come here and see everything we do and are overwhelmed," said Art Ayris, the church's minister of evangelism and ministry as well as the CCC administrator. "But we started right where we were. We tell people to focus on the needs in their community and start right where they are. Now we have the Ministry Village, but each of these ministries began in an old house. We put the ministries in there and ministered to people out of those houses. Our suggestion to others is to start where you are. Give food out of a closet in your church. Work with women and children in the locations where they are."

"But for some of the ministries (the church is now doing), there's not a place to go, so we've just had to learn the hard way," he said.

First Baptist Church members began putting down on paper what they had learned about ministry from doing ministry. Those experiences and principles were written in a manual on ministry evangelism. A book Roesel co-authored with Donald Atkinson, *Meeting Needs, Sharing Christ: Ministry Evangelism in Today's New Testament Church,* was released in 1995 by LifeWay Press in Nashville. The book is being translated into Portuguese for use in Brazil.

Still on the drawing board is a hospitality house, where people from other churches can stay while observing the work in the Ministry Village. That idea was born out of the church's annual ministry evangelism conferences. People attend from all over the United States. Now the congregation has been designated a teaching church by the Florida Baptist Convention, a place where people can learn firsthand how to do ministry evangelism.

Roesel says ministry evangelism is a "passion for the lost and a purpose for the church." He described the "beauty of ministry evangelism" as "a bullet that fits any gun. Even the smallest church can reach out through ministry. The church may not be able to welcome the whole city with ten thousand loaves of bread, but it can have one person welcome one person with one loaf."

The Leesburg church's ministry book lists more than one hundred ministries that churches can do. Roesel said that churches not involved in ministry evangelism "are missing the privilege—the most effective way ever seen for reaching people for Jesus Christ."

"Twenty years ago we would have been criticized" for the emphasis on social concerns, Roesel said, "because it would have been called the social Gospel, which was all social and no Gospel. But this is not the old social Gospel—this is ministry evangelism. I exist for evangelism as fire exists for burning. Every single ministry we do has the goal of reaching hurting people with the Gospel of Jesus Christ."

Roesel calls the needs in Leesburg exhausting. Prior to the church's emphasis on ministry-based evangelism, the congregation had "blitzed, surveyed, done everything we could do" to get prospects. The pastor said that more church people were involved in weekly visitation than they had prospects to visit.

"But once we became involved in ministry evangelism, we had people coming out of the woodwork—coming from everywhere," he said. "Whatever the ministry, it's just amazing the needs. We have a cross section of every problem found in the United States. No area is immune anymore. We may be in the 'Bible Belt' but Satan is having a heyday. I've never seen so many hurting people. As long as you minister to hurting people, you'll never lack for an audience. It's amazing that in a town the size of Leesburg we have this much work to do. There's not a place—town, village, one-store country place—that doesn't have the problems we have right here."

Roesel said that God "began laying on my heart nearly twenty years ago" the concept of ministry evangelism. He has been pastor of the Leesburg church for twenty-two years.

"God orchestrated the whole thing," Roesel said. "At first I didn't know what was going on—some need would crop up, and we would meet it. Then I saw what God was doing, and the vision became almost an obsession with me."

Roesel called trained leaders the key to ministry. He said a seminary student once asked him what was the greatest mistake he had ever made. "A thousand things came to mind," Roesel remembered, "but God gave me and him the same answer at the same time. The greatest mistake I ever made was when I had the idea that I was the only one who was able to do anything. On the other hand, the greatest move was when I stepped aside and let the laymen do what they could do far better than I could."

"I've never seen anything explode like this," he said 'of the church's ministry. "It's just awesome. God has raised up the staff through and from the congregation."

Roesel admitted that some church members initially resisted the idea of reaching undesirables in society. There were those who said, "These aren't our kind of people." Others said, "I don't like to have my wife walk by these kinds of people to get into the church."

But Roesel said those attitudes changed about eighteen years ago.

"Now I'm afraid to mention a ministry unless I mean business because the people will automatically go for it," he said. For instance, Roesel said he was "just testing the waters" on ministry to people with AIDS when "the deacons came with a unanimous voice, saying, 'If this comes up in our community, let's go for it.' " Likewise, a drug rehabilitation center is also in the works. The two newest projects in which the Leesburg church has become involved are a school of fine arts and a hospital ministry. The fine arts ministry teaches everything from violin to creative movement. "It reaches a cross section of the city since we have started the only fine arts school in the area," Roesel said. "We have many people bringing their children, providing just another opportunity for a Gospel witness."

Roesel said that the city hospital called the church, offering a registered nurse and malpractice insurance if the congregation would furnish a facility. That medical care ministry has been operating for a year now. The church is investigating the possibility of building a new clinic in its Ministry Village, staffed by two nurses.

"This may become the pilot project for ministry of this type across the nation because it's a win-win situation," Roesel said. "It saves the hospital a small fortune because we can provide care for ten cents on the dollar, and it provides us the opportunity to bear witness to everyone who comes. We're meeting the medical needs of transients and those who can't afford hospital care." Roesel said the hospital called the church because the administrators "knew we care about people." He said that's how ministry literally explodes.

"From Genesis to Revelation, the theme is ministry evangelism," Roesel said. "If you want that which will reach people for Jesus Christ, sweeten your fellowship, and double your budget, then give yourself away through ministry evangelism."

After moving into the Women's Care Center, Charlotte Rubush started attending AA meetings and found a full-time job at an assisted living facility for Alzheimer patients. Things were going well until her boyfriend started showing up at work. As a result, she lost her job and relapsed into her drug use. After three days, Charlotte returned to the center, where, instead of condemnation and rejection, she found mercy and grace.

Shortly afterward, Charlotte gave her life to Jesus and has remained clean since. She also began attending First Baptist Church, Leesburg. Over the next few months she went through additional drug rehabilitation and secured steady employment. The administrator at the assisted living facility who fired her called and offered another full-time position. Charlotte has since been promoted to resident director and placed in charge of resident care and personnel.

"There have been so many blessings," she noted. "After nine months, I moved out of the center and into my own apartment. I attended financial counseling classes at First Baptist Church and was able to pay off the mountain of fines and debts I had accumulated. I have a car that was donated by a member of First Baptist Church, and my children will be coming to live with me when school is out this summer. Today, I am drug free, debt free, and spiritually free—and he whom Christ sets free is free indeed!"

Charlotte came to the Lord through the ministry evangelism of First Baptist Church, Leesburg, and she has since become very active in the church's outreach. She teaches a weekly Bible study at the Women's Care Center and relieves the housemother when she needs time off. Charlotte also serves as treasurer and outreach worker at the Highway Church, a cross-cultural ministry of First Baptist Church. In addition, Charlotte volunteers with the Child Care Ministry on Sunday mornings.

"I can never express the love and gratitude I feel for First Baptist Church and the Women's Care Center," Charlotte said. "The love and support I have received over the past two years is extraordinary. But most of all I am grateful to God for His love and the gift of my salvation. I give the Lord the glory for the changes in my life because I know they came to me only because of Him."

Discussion

1. Richard Gorski writes, "Our experience is that truly effective presentations of the Gospel are those that are made in the context of a relationship which will provide multiple opportunities to talk about Christ." How can you benefit from that insight?

2. What can be done to make a Bible study more hospitable for the stranger?

3. What can be done to make the worship setting more hospitable for the stranger?

4. Which event from Keith Wright's monthly list could your group implement? Your congregation?

5. How can you reach out to international students with your practice of hospitality?

6. How does Deuteronomy 10:17–21 speak to the issues of hospitality?

7. What other ideas from this session do you think your congregation could implement? You personally? Your community?